Nostrum Conspiracy

Robert Grant

Copyright 2015 Robert Grant
All rights reserved.
ISBN-13: 978-0-9906654-2-7
Library of Congress Control Number: 2015917320

NT Publishing Company
119 Evergreen Road
Suite 43572
Louisville, KY 40253-0572
www.NTPublishingCompany.com

This title is also available in eBook.

The names, characters, and events depicted in this story are the fictitious creations of the author, and any resemblance to persons, living or dead, is purely coincidental. Product names, brands, and other trademarks referred to within this book are the property of their respective trade mark holders. Unless specified, no association between the author and any trademark holder is expressed or implied. Use of a term in this book should not be regarded as affecting the validity of any trademark, registered trademark, or service mark.

No part of this publication may be reproduced in any form, stored in any retrieval system, posted on any website, or transmitted in any form or by any means including, digital, electronic, scanning, photocopy, recording, or otherwise, without the express written permission from the publisher, except for brief quotations in printed reviews and articles.

Please remember to leave a review of *Nostrum Conspiracy* at your favorite retailer.

Read *Naked Tao* and *UnderBelly* by Robert Grant
Great Mother to be released soon.

What Others are Saying About
The Nostrum Conspiracy

"Robert Grant is a master story teller…combines nonstop action with a touch of Far Eastern mysticism…" M. Wexler

"You've written something special…" D. Bruner.

"…my fave author, Robert Grant. I ask you to give Nostrum Conspiracy an earnest looksee! This brilliant mind will have you traveling about to places such as the Amazon Rainforest…his descriptions of the unusual cast of characters will leave you breathless with delight." D. Summers.

ALSO BY ROBERT GRANT

DEDICATION

This is dedicated to Kevin Akers
and Gia-Fu Feng, may you party in the
coral colored clouds with the immortals.

BULK PURCHASES

We will gladly provide paperback copies of this book at a discounted price for bulk purchases. Send a request to Robert@NTPublishingCompany.com.

PROLOGUE

Somewhere in a remote part of the Himalayas is a small monastery. It was carefully designed by ancient craftsmen skilled in the art of feng shui. Clever engineers positioned it on a small ledge halfway up the face of a mountain.

They took advantage of the mountain's perpetual misty cloud cover to keep it hidden from the world. Miles of bewildering canyons make it inaccessible to all except the initiated. Indistinguishable from the rock from which it is carved, only a few know of its existence. The resident monks call it Sovereigns' Refuge.

It is a place lost to time, as if time does not exist. Still, on this day two cloaked figures quietly stand on the east terrace watching the morning sun peek between two misty mountains.

It is a woman's voice that breaks the silence.

"It is time."

CHAPTER 1

An instant turns into the tragedy of a lifetime when a bullet tears a pinky sized hole into the forehead of the woman you love. It is especially painful when you've spent a lifetime ignoring her.

I allowed a single tear to follow the path of least resistance to the corner of my mouth, before wiping it with the tip of the tongue. Savoring the slight burn from the salt, I tried to remember the last time I wept. No luck there. I'm sure I've cried before. A man would have to be emotionally bankrupt to have never cried.

I've been such a jerk, but there's one thing I know for sure, this is the first time I've shed a tear of joy. Ginny is alive. I don't know how, but she is alive. Somehow she survived the gun shot and still looks radiant. By comparison, I feel like I've been kicked by an ornery mule.

Ginny doesn't need the clothes her company designs to make her beautiful. Even in a flimsy hospital gown, she is stunning. Tall and athletic, her flawless legs led the eye upward toward a tight little behind, while waves of soft dark brown hair fell gracefully onto her broad swimmer's shoulders spotted with a few freckles despite her olive skin tone.

Her eyes sparkle with life. Even though I've known her as long as I can remember, I find their color difficult to pinpoint. It is an unusual shade of blue or green that is best described as the color of a tropical sea.

The rest of Ginny's face is equally magnificent. She has an aristocratic high bridged nose set between wide cheekbones that narrow into a high forehead. It is a beautiful face that is enhanced with the flush of radiant good health. You might even say all true beauty is a reflection of good health.

As happy as I was to see her like this, I thought I might be hallucinating. The last time I saw her she was lying in a pool of her own blood, pale and lifeless. Yet now I find her in a hospital bed, the model of good health. How the hell is that possible?

"You're alive," said Ginny.

I shook my head as if that would wipe away any illusions. Still, there was no mistaking her musical voice. It was time to test the waters.

"You died," I murmured.

"I knew Slotter was going to pull the trigger before she did," said Ginny. "Everything happened so slowly. When the hammer fell I only had one thought…deflect that bullet. I knew, without a doubt, I could do it…but I failed."

Kim Slotter was a war hero gone bad. She had kidnapped Ginny and held her at an abandoned warehouse in the wrong end of town. I took a ragtag group and tried to rescue her, but the heroic deed went south and we were shot by the bad guys.

"You succeeded in deflecting the bullet, but that shot was intended for me, not you," I said.

Ginny absentmindedly massaged the spot just above her heart. Without thinking I mirrored her movement and felt the bandages covering the exit wound. I was lucky. If the bullet had been slightly lower it would have killed me.

"You're wounded," she said. "I failed."

She thought only of protecting me and damn near got herself killed doing it. Without thinking, I gathered her into my arms and held her tight.

I had never done anything so rash in my life and had a moment where I thought maybe I had overstepped a boundary between us. The moment of doubt passed when Ginny melted into me like she had been there a thousand times before.

"You did not fail," I said. "It wasn't Slotter who did this to me. I was shot in the back by one of her minions."

The brush with death opened my eyes to a few

things. Introspection has an annoying way of doing that. The thing that hurt the most as we lay together in an expanding puddle of blood was the regret.

I couldn't understand why I had ignored Ginny all of those years. None of the reasons that once seemed adequate withstood the test of final judgment as we faced death together.

After the wave of grief passed, I wiped the tears from her shoulder and reminded myself that somehow she was miraculously alive and well. The grief was replaced with self-doubt. She couldn't still be alive. I must be dreaming, or worse, experiencing a psychotic break.

Neither was acceptable and I was thinking of giving myself a good hard pinch, when our tender moment was interrupted by a disapproving voice.

"What do you think you're doing?"

A young nurse with a fake smile plastered across her face stormed into the room. Her dirty blond hair had been hastily smoothed back, leaving a few stubborn strands that refused to comply. Instead, they curled around a flushed cheek, as testament to her refusal to follow the straight and narrow. On the opposite side of her face, a streak of dark mascara ran a quarter-inch from the corner of her left eye.

She was dressed in rumpled surgical scrubs and the buttons on her top were out of alignment. She smelled of sweat from a quick tryst in some dark corner of the hospital.

Her name tag identified her as Nurse Nightshade. She was trying hard to be perky, but failed miserably. I had the sense Nurse Nightshade was trained to be upbeat, but it didn't come naturally to her. It was obvious she wasn't pleased with me.

"This patient is in critical condition," she said coldly. "I'm going to change her bandage and afterwards you need to leave so she can get some rest."

For someone charged with patient care, she was shockingly unobservant. She hadn't once looked at Ginny and seemed content to glare at me instead.

I nodded toward Ginny. Nurse Nightshade followed my eyes. At first she didn't seem to register what was in front of her, but when it finally sunk in that Ginny was the model of good health, she muffled a small scream with her hand.

"That's impossible," gasped Nurse Nightshade. "She's at death's door and Doctor Wiemp doesn't expect her to make it through the night."

It irked me that she gave more weight to what the Doctor said than what her own eyes revealed about Ginny's condition. Clearly, she was not at death's door. Ginny was alive and well.

I wanted to point this out to her, but resisted the temptation.

Instead I asked, "How do you explain it then…a miracle maybe?"

Nurse Nightshade ignored my question. Instead she made the sign of the cross, as if that would somehow protect her from something she didn't understand. I can't be certain, but I think I also heard her whisper something about God's own miracle.

I wasn't serious about the miracle comment, but that didn't seem to matter much to her. Once she completed the religious rituals, her nurses' training took over and she busied herself with Ginny's bandage.

At first she seemed hesitant, as if she feared what lay beneath it. Her fear didn't last long before she made up her mind to do her job and began to slowly remove the blood crusted dressing.

While she fussed with the bandage, I turned to ask Pony Tail what he knew about Ginny's condition, but he was nowhere in sight. Weird, I thought. He had been dressed in nurse's scrubs and hovering over Ginny when I walked into the room a few minutes earlier. I sure didn't hear him leave.

"Maybe the other nurse knows what happened to Ginny," I said to Nurse Nightshade.

Her attention was on the bandage and I wasn't sure if she heard me at first. I was about to repeat it when she finally answered.

"I'm the only one working this shift," she said.

"There was a male nurse in here a few minutes ago," I said.

Since she ignored me, I added a description of Pony Tail to give her memory a boost.

"He's in his mid-twenties, medium height, brown skin, and blond hair," I said.

I still didn't get a response from her, so I lamely continued with the description in the hopes something would register with her.

"He wears his hair long, but tied back in a ponytail," I said. "You can't miss him."

Nurse Nightshade was rude, but she was also working so I didn't take it personally. Besides, her focus was on carefully removing Ginny's bandages and I didn't want to distract her. It almost felt random when she finally responded with a shake of her head.

"There's no one like that here," she said.

I gave up on Pony Tail and chalked it up as one more strange mystery to follow-up at a later time.

While the nurse fussed with the bandages I took a moment to look around the room. Hospital rooms are places where I put on horse blinders, since it's best not to see too much. The rooms tend to be stark and filled with unpleasant odors. For the most part, Ginny's room was no exception. However, it did have one interesting feature that drew my eye.

An odd picture hung on the wall next to the bathroom. Most art work in hospital rooms is virtually invisible, but this one caught my eye. It was a wreath, but I saw something odd hidden in its design. I could very clearly see a snake eating a bird. It appeared to be the same symbol vandals painted on Ch'ing's wall.

Ch'ing is my martial arts teacher who mysteriously disappeared a few days ago. When we searched his house for him, we found it had been vandalized. For some unknown reason, they had spray painted the snake eating bird symbol on the wall along with the message, "It has begun."

Nurse Nightshade removed the last of the bandages and gasped. Since she was obstructing my view, I craned my neck to see around her, but still couldn't see a thing.

I wasn't sure what to expect. I know I saw Slotter blow a hole in her forehead and a sick part of me wanted that hole to be there, so I wouldn't have to face the possibility I was crazy. The rest of me wanted Ginny's forehead to be as smooth as a baby's butt.

When Nurse Nightshade finally shifted

positions, what I saw was a bit of dried blood that she wiped away. Where there was once a hole the size of my little finger, now there was only smooth healthy skin. There was no evidence Ginny had suffered an injury.

I was relieved for sure, but now I doubted my memory of the events at the warehouse. Was Ginny really taken by an ex-special forces renegade and held hostage in a warehouse in West Louisville?

A group of us went to rescue her, but all hell broke loose. I was shot. Ginny was shot. The only family I had left was trapped on the roof of a burning building. I don't know how Uncle Jim could have survived those flames. Oh…and my crazy macaw, Bird, went down underneath a tank of a man.

The only person I care about who managed to get through it unharmed was my best friend, Eric. When I awoke in the hospital, I found him sitting at my bedside. It should have been comforting, but Eric was behaving strangely. He seemed worried about more than recent events, but wouldn't say what it was.

Then it got even weirder when my attorney, showed up with a Marine Colonel in tow. The Colonel is in charge of some hush-hush military investigation involving Slotter, the special forces renegade who shot Ginny.

They offered me a deal to avoid prosecution for two murders I didn't commit. One of the dead men was my boss, John Biggs, who was found hanging from the chandelier in his posh corner office after he got a call from a federal prosecutor.

I'm a lawyer, by the way. At least I was before the firm placed me on unpaid leave. A spendthrift spouse and strangling medical bills for my mother's long term healthcare have left me broke. So, I took a job working as a body guard for a monk named Padma Ganesha.

He wrote a bestselling book about the happiest place on Earth. Ginny somehow persuaded him to travel to Louisville and speak at a lecture series called, "Ideas to Change the World." It was held in an auditorium on Louisville's waterfront called, the Center. When I arrived, I found the security guard with a knife buried in his chest.

The evening went from bad to worse after Pony Tail started shooting. Thirty-two hundred peace loving hippies fought their way to the exits, only to find themselves locked inside. They are all dead now. According to the news reports, there was a gas leak, but I was told by the Marine Colonel the gas leak is a cover story.

For some reason, the military wanted to cover up the truth and offered me immunity to keep quiet about what really happened. The deal was a huge insult to my intelligence. Even though I was in no mood to allow myself to be controlled by some military goon, I went along with it to get rid of them.

As soon as the Colonel left my room, I slipped out in the hopes of finding Slotter in the intensive care unit recovering from her own gunshot wounds. Following Slotter's arrest, a police detective stuck a pistol in her belly and pulled the trigger. The Jack Ruby moment was motivated by vengeance for the death of the detective's daughter at the Center.

Slotter had made a few enemies and we all wanted her dead, but it was beginning to look like she was under the protection of the same Colonel who was trying to hush up what really happened at the Center.

Instead of Slotter, I found Ginny alive and well in the intensive care unit. I thought for sure she was dead and now I was beginning to doubt my own memory of what happened. It was inconceivable that she took a bullet to the head and survived, let alone healed so quickly. At least it was inconceivable to a sane person.

I shook off the self-doubt. Something was amiss, but if Ginny survived by some unknown miracle, then maybe, just maybe, Uncle Jim and Bird also survived. I could only hope, but for now I wanted to focus on what was right in front of me. Ginny was alive and that was huge.

Neither the nurse nor I knew what to say in response to the sight of her perfectly healed wound. It was Ginny who broke the silence.

"My father is still alive and I'm going to find him," said Ginny. "Will you help me, Grant?"

Ginny's father had disappeared years ago. For some reason, Slotter thought he was still alive and that's why she kidnapped Ginny. In some weird way, it must have given Ginny hope. I didn't think for a minute the man was still alive after all this time, but I wanted to be with Ginny and she wanted to search for him.

"Of course I will," I answered. "Where do you want to begin?"

"Brazil…he was last seen boarding a small plane for a tour of the Amazon Rainforest," answered Ginny without hesitation. "We'll begin there."

"That's a long time for someone to be missing," I said.

"I've never given up hope that my father is alive," she said. "One of the many reasons I opened a factory in Brazil was to pick up where the police left off with their investigation into his disappearance."

"What did they tell you?" I asked.

"Only that he charted a small plane and it never returned," she said.

"Where was it chartered?" I asked.

"Manaus, at the mouth of the Amazon," she answered.

"The Amazon Rainforest is huge," I said. "Do you know where he was headed?"

She shrugged.

"Nobody seems to know," said Ginny.

Something was bothering me about this story, but I couldn't quite put my finger on it. There were pieces of the puzzle missing and I had a nagging feeling I knew something about them.

"Do they know where the plane went down?" I asked.

"No," answered Ginny. "They spent a few days looking for the wreckage, but soon gave up when it couldn't be spotted from the air."

"Do you have plan?" I asked.

She nodded, but before she could answer, the nurse hit the emergency call button.

"You don't just walk out of ICU," barked Nurse Nightshade. "You're not going anywhere until Dr. Wiemp releases you."

Ginny stiffened. She looked like she was about to give the nurse a piece of her mind. I don't know about Ginny, but I don't like to be told what I can or can't do, especially by a stranger.

Still, no good ever comes from an unnecessary confrontation over something that is easily resolved. It was time for diplomacy, but before I could speak, Ginny snapped at the nurse.

"I'm not your prisoner," said Ginny.

Nurse Nightshade puffed her flat chest out as far as it would go.

"Rules are rules," she said. "You have to see the Doctor first."

"Not if she doesn't want to," I said. "As you can see, she's in perfect health."

The nurse shook her head.

"Who are you and what are you doing in my ICU outside of visiting hours?" she demanded.

Her attitude stunned me. It was time to kick it up a notch, so I extended my hand to her.

"My name is Grant Li, Attorney-at-Law," I said. "This woman does not need your permission to leave. Surely it's not your intention to hold her against her will."

Nurse Nightshade shrank from the extended hand, as if it held a poisonous snake. She opened her mouth to speak, but then abruptly shut it again. I think she was accustomed to patients following orders and our rebellion unbalanced her.

Between my martial arts training and law practice, I know a fighter when I see one. Nurse Nightshade was a fighter and wasn't about to lose a conflict with a couple of patients. She shifted her focus to the hospital gown I wore and somehow managed to regain her sense of power.

"You are a patient in this hospital and there is blood seeping from your bandages," said the nurse. "Let's get you back to your room before you hurt yourself."

I wasn't feeling my best and the bed rest she offered was tempting, but her tone annoyed me. I was about to say something I might regret when I heard footsteps outside of the door.

An arrogant voice barked a little too loudly, "This better be a real emergency."

A wave of relief passed over Nurse Nightshade's face. She could now pass the torch to someone else and that somebody happened to be wearing a name tag that identified him as, Jonathan Wiemp, M.D.

Dr. Wiemp was tall, but seemed much shorter thanks to a pronounced stoop. In addition to the stoop, he had a sag in the back of his neck that reminded me of a cartoon vulture I had seen one Saturday morning years ago.

In sharp contrast to an exceptionally pointed chin, he had a wide forehead with four rows of deep wrinkles spread across it. Thinning hair and grayish skin, gave him a haggard look.

It didn't get any better as you moved downward. A pot belly pushed the waist band of his slacks to the max. I didn't get a sense that the doctor took very good care of himself.

I guessed he was much younger than he appeared, but his clothes didn't help him look his age. They were old fashioned and added to his antique appearance. From the faded bow tie, to the heavily worn wing tip shoes, he looked like he had been wearing the same outfit since 1958.

Nurse Nightshade must have seen something different in Dr. Wiemp, because she never once took her doe eyed gaze from him. On the other hand, Dr. Wiemp hardly looked at her. My feelings about her softened considerably when I realized it would eventually end badly for her.

"This patient wants to leave, Doctor," said the nurse.

Dr. Wiemp scowled over the top of black rimmed glasses at Ginny. Leaving was not part of his prognosis. He expected her to be dead by morning. I saw something else in his face. This arrogant man disliked being wrong and found her recovery insulting.

"No one is leaving," said Dr. Wiemp in a raspy voice that told me he was a heavy smoker.

I had one of those random moments we all have from time to time. For some odd reason, Dr. Wiemp's statement reminded me of the title to Jim Morrison's biography, "No One Here Gets Out Alive." The disturbing comparison was all I needed to abandon diplomacy and shift into full blown lawyer mode.

"Unless you step aside and allow her to leave, you will be prosecuted to the fullest extent of the law for false imprisonment," I said to Dr. Wiemp.

He looked me up and down before digging a hand into his pocket and pulling out a smartphone. He punched in a call and waited impatiently.

"We have a problem," he said into the phone. "Send security."

"Has everyone gone completely insane?" asked Ginny.

"This is ridiculous," I agreed. "We're leaving."

I took Ginny's hand and gently pulled her to her feet. At first, she submitted, but then looked down at her clothes. I followed her eyes. She was wearing one of those awful hospital gowns that invariably expose the patient's behind. In most instances, it's a behind I'd rather not look at, but as Ginny cut a path to the closet I enjoyed a lingering look at a backside that was flawless in a Barbie doll sort of way.

I had seen her in a bikini a few days earlier and hungered for more. I watched as she stuffed her things into a bag and grabbed my hand again.

As we headed to the door, I caught a glimpse of the nurse's hateful glare. She quickly cut her jealous eyes to Dr. Wiemp, who was standing in the door blocking our way. He didn't show any signs of yielding.

I looked straight into his eyes and with dead calm said, "You need to step aside, now."

Dr. Wiemp's arrogance seemed to dissipate. For the first time, he was unsure of himself. His eyes faltered and his gaze dropped to his feet as he stepped aside. I led Ginny into the hall where we ran smack into two huge security guards.

Dr. Wiemp's arrogance returned as he barked, "Take this man to the psychological services unit and put him in restraints."

Of all the things he could have said, Dr. Wiemp managed to say the only thing that could send me over the edge. Raw terror pushed me into berserker mode. In keeping with my training, I savagely attacked the biggest guard first, delivering multiple blows to his vital points within the first three seconds.

He was out cold and on his way to the ground when I disarmed the second security guard and pressed the 45 to his temple. I would have pulled the trigger too, but I heard something in Ginny's voice that pulled me from the brink.

"Oh, my God!" said Ginny. "Grant, no…please don't!"

Her voice saved the guard's life and it saved me from doing something that would have haunted me for the rest of my life. In the face of what might have been my hands started shaking uncontrollably. When I turned to Ginny, I was crushed by what I saw in her eyes. I wanted to explain and took a deep breath to gather myself, but felt something stab me in the neck and then I was out cold.

CHAPTER 2

My throat was dry. I tried to swallow. Nothing happened. Panicked, I tried again and again without success. I was suffocating. That would end it for sure.

"He's waking up," said a man with a kind voice.

A woman with a hard edge to her voice said, "Good, prep him for his therapy session."

"Are you sure he can handle it?" asked the man. "He's not very strong."

"If you want to keep your job nurse, you will never presume to question me again," snarled the woman.

"Yes doctor," he said.

The woman scared me. Still, a part of me was curious about the nurse. His voice was kind. I wanted to open my eyes so I could get a look at him, but they were clinched tight and refused to budge.

Everything was dark. I heard footsteps. A door opened and shut.

The man said, "Don't be afraid young man, it will be over soon."

He loosened the straps restraining my arms and rubbed my wrists to get the circulation going. The massage moved to my legs. The doctor's hands were different from his. Hers were hard and cold, but his were gentle and warm.

"Can we walk today?" he asked.

I wanted to answer him, but couldn't. It wasn't safe. Better to stay inside…away from people, especially the Fat Lady. I needed to stay away from her. She wanted to hurt me. It was her fault I was in this terrible place where bad people hurt me. There wasn't anyone I could trust.

Strong arms moved me from the warm hospital bed to a cold gurney.

"Should we open our eyes today?" asked the man.

I vigorously shook my head. I didn't want to see the terrible things they were about to do to me.

The nurse used his fingers to comb my hair back. When he finished, he paused a moment before pushing the gurney out the door and down the hall toward the therapy room. At least that's what they called it. After the first therapy session it was the "Bad Place" to me.

The Bad Place smelled like burnt hair and pee. I shivered from the cold…and the fear. The doctor ordered me to be still. Her voice echoed slightly in the cavernous room. I knew what she would do to me if I didn't comply and willed myself still. I hoped the goose bumps had the good sense to cooperate too.

I resisted the urge to scream as Sadistic Doctor strapped me to a cold narrow table. Next she taped electrodes to my forehead and ordered me to open my mouth wide, but then didn't give me a chance to comply before roughly jamming a mouth plug between my teeth.

"The meds interfere with the therapy, so we'll skip them," she said. "You are a broken little boy who needs the full treatment. Still, I don't have any hope that it will work for the likes of you."

That's what she always said right before she sent electricity jolting through me. The doctor said it wouldn't hurt, but it did. It hurt so bad I wanted to die…tried to die, but death never came. Instead, I'd shake real bad and then pass out. I know that's what I did, because she told me. It made her mad when I didn't stay awake, but I didn't care.

I awoke in a cold sweat. Slowly, I opened my eyes and looked around. The room was different…more modern than before, but I knew I was back there again. This time I wanted to see my tormentors…to look them in the eye and let them see I was unafraid.

The door opened and a determined looking

woman stepped inside. I caught a glimpse of Dr. Wiemp in the hall. He was talking in low tones to a short, balding man wearing an Italian designer suit that must have cost a small fortune.

It was a different suit, but I'd recognize Mr. Suit anywhere. I bumped into him in the hallway of my law office and sent him sliding across the polished marble floor like an air hockey puck. Moments later, I discovered my boss gasping for his last breath while hanging by the neck from a tacky chandelier. What was he doing here?

The door closed and a shadow filled its place. The dark woman was topped with witchy black hair and matching circles around her eyes. She had tried to fill the deep craggy lines in her face with makeup, and then tried to offset the paleness with rouge painted on her cheeks and lips. The end result was hideous.

She wore the same sensible shoes I remembered from twenty years ago….square toed, black patent leather, laced up and tied with a perfect little bow. Dark pantyhose covered chicken legs sticking out of the bottom of a straight black skirt that hung exactly two inches below the knee.

Her white lab coat was the only thing she wore that wasn't black. Even it was somehow dominated by the top of the black pen sticking out of her pocket and the black and chrome stethoscope hanging around her neck. The name tag pinned to her lab coat identified her as "Doctor." I would have added the word, "Sadistic," but that's just my opinion.

Sadistic Doctor had aged thirty in the last twenty, but it was still the same hateful face I saw gloating over me. I was back in hell, but this time I was a full-grown man. Stronger than before and I wasn't about to show this bitch any fear.

"I always knew you'd be back," said Sadistic Doctor. "We never finished your treatment plan and look what it got us...two innocent men savagely attacked."

All the rage buried inside of me came to the surface. I wanted to hurt her like she once hurt me. The only thing that kept me from her throat was the restraints tied to my wrists and ankles. Restraints or not, I tried to break free.

"He has learned to rattle the cage," she mocked.

I glared at her and said, "I'm not a helpless little boy anymore."

Something in my eyes gave her a moment's pause. As she pondered what she saw, the door opened and Mr. Suit walked into the room. Sadistic Doctor reluctantly pulled her cold eyes from her prey and gave the intruder a slight nod of recognition.

There was a subtle change in her demeanor, as well. Mr. Suit's body language told me he was accustomed to being in charge and the scowl on Sadistic Doctor's face was all I needed to know she didn't like it one bit. He made a dismissive movement with his hand. She looked as if she might argue the point with him, but then seemed to think better of it and left the room in a huff.

"Who are you?" I asked.

For a moment, it looked like he might tell me, but then he gave a small shake of the head and changed the subject.

"I want to assure you," said Mr. Suit, "that we will keep you here as long as necessary."

"You won't be able to hold me more than seventy-two hours," I said. "When I get out, you will regret this."

He smirked.

"How do you know we haven't already kept you strapped to that table for weeks?" he asked.

That gave me reason to pause. I had no way of knowing how long they had kept me drugged and unconscious. There should have been a quick hearing before a Judge, but I sure didn't remember one.

"What do you want from me?" I asked.

"First, we want you to return the confidential files you stole from us," he answered.

I didn't expect that answer and had no idea

what he was talking about. I didn't have what Mr. Suit wanted, but maybe I could use this to my advantage. I wasn't exactly sure how, but I decided to string him along for the time being.

"I'm not sure what you're talking about," I said.

Mr. Suit stroked his power tie. It looked to me like he was choosing his next words very carefully.

"We know you have our property," he said. "If you return it, we will reward you. If you keep it, then we will hurt you until you break. Once you are broken, you will give us our property and the only reward you'll get is all the pain you needlessly suffered."

His threats didn't scare me. I had endured electroshock treatments as a small boy and figured I could handle them now.

I now knew that these files were the real reason I was tied to this hospital bed and they were willing to torture me to recover them. It was time to find out what else I could learn from Mr. Suit.

"You said the first thing you wanted was your confidential files," I said. "What else do you want?"

"We want to know where he is hiding," said Mr. Suit.

This was the second time in the last few days

that the bad guys used extreme measures to find someone. The last time it happened, Kim Slotter, was looking for Ginny's father. That did not end well.

"Who are you talking about?" I asked.

"Your little girlfriend's father," he answered.

I wasn't sure how her father was connected to all of this, but the bad guys seemed to be willing to do anything to find him. Warfare is about deception. It's best to keep your enemies guessing as long as possible. I decided to play dumb and keep Mr. Suit guessing about me. Besides, I didn't want these people to ever think they could use Ginny as leverage against me.

"I'm a married man," I said.

"Don't play me, Mr. Li," he said. "We both know your marriage has tanked and now you're seeing Virginia Bardough."

"She's an old friend," I said. "She's certainly not my girlfriend. Other than a few days ago, I hadn't seen her for years."

"Where's her father?" demanded Mr. Suit.

"He's dead," I answered. "Why are you searching for a dead man?"

Before he could answer, the door burst open and Eric stormed in.

Pushing Mr. Suit aside, he said, "Get out of the way fat boy. I'm taking Grant and we're leaving this God forsaken place."

Eric and I have been friends since we were kids running barefoot all summer. We went to the same school, played football, and even studied martial arts together. We were more like brothers than anything and always had each other's backs. Boy was I ever glad to see him.

If Mr. Suit was surprised to see Eric storm into the room, he didn't show it. Instead, he puffed out his chest and demanded that Eric leave immediately or he would have him arrested.

In response to the threat, Eric quickly closed the gap between them and crushed Mr. Suit with a hard right hand to the jaw. Mr. Suit had one of those square chins you see on tough guys in Hollywood films. The jaw shattered like cheap glass and his arrogant eyes rolled back an instant before he crumbled unconscious to the floor.

Eric loves a good fight, but the easy victory over Mr. Suit hardly qualified. Still, the way Eric gloated over his limp body reminded me of Muhammad Ali towering over Sonny Liston. For some reason he seemed to take special pleasure in kicking Mr. Suit's butt. I have to admit, it felt good to see that happen, but I think it would have been better if it had been the Sadistic Doctor instead…woman or not.

When it dawned on Eric that Mr. Suit was hardly worth gloating over, he turned to me and said, "Damn, don't you look freaky…all strapped down and submissive like."

He must of seen I was in no mood for jokes, because he quickly added, "The straps look tight, but you could stand to do some work on the submissive part."

"Unstrap me," I growled.

"Awe, lighten up dude," said Eric.

It is hard to be upset with Eric for long. His good nature is genuine and he wears it on his sleeve like a proud trademark. Take his shit eating grin, for example. It says in no uncertain terms he could care less what you think of him.

In addition to his winning smile, it doesn't hurt that Eric is blessed with classic Hollywood good looks and a male stripper's body. Chicks love him. Frankly, I can't see what all the fuss is about, but that might just be me.

Eric is one of those friendly fun loving guys who have never met a stranger. When you couple his winning personality with pretty-boy good looks, it's not hard to understand why he's usually surrounded by a crowd of groupies…mostly female.

Even though women of all ages are forever hitting on me, I'm no ladies man. Casual is just not my thing. I'm looking for depth and that isn't as easy to find as you might think. So many of these women just seem to be looking for one thing and it's not my heart.

Their approach varies in the details, but the thrust of it is always the same. They open with a lame line like, "I always wanted to get me a big hunk of yummy chocolate, like you," and then it goes downhill from there.

Hell, I'm not even full blooded African-American. You might say I'm an all American mutt...a mix of several diverse blood lines, including Chinese, African-American, and a good measure of U.S. Grant...the dead President on the fifty dollar bill.

I sighed. Eric grinned.

"Let's get you home where you're free to engage in all kinds of kinkiness," he said.

"Not my thing," I said.

"I'm just trying to help a friend get over a bad marriage," he said.

"What I need right now is to get out this place," I said.

"That we can do," said Eric.

"I'm not leaving without Ginny," I said. "Let's go get her."

Eric's demeanor changed radically. Suddenly, everything in the room was more interesting than me. He was hiding something and I was in no mood to pry it out of him.

"What is it now, Eric?" I asked.

He recognized my tone of voice and abandoned his usual irreverent attitude. He cleared his throat, started to speak, stopped, and then cleared it a second time as if he missed an obstruction the first time around.

Finally, he mumbled, "Umm…she's gone, Grant, and I don't think she wants you to follow."

CHAPTER 3

Eric released the straps securing me to the hospital bed, but refused to say anything else about Ginny. On the one hand, I was grateful for the rescue, but he had been behaving strangely lately and it was beginning to take a toll on our friendship.

In addition to whatever he was hiding about Ginny, there was the bungled rescue attempt. When I needed his help, he didn't show-up. As a result, Uncle Jim was trapped in a burning building, Ginny and I were shot, and Bird was smashed underneath a tank of a guy. I was starting to have some nagging doubts about him.

"Where were you?" I demanded.

Eric looked a bit sheepish as he answered, "It took us a while to find you."

"We didn't have any trouble finding it," I accused.

He stared at me long and hard as if he wanted to be sure he said and did the right thing.

"One minute you were in a hospital bed and the next you were gone," he said. "We figured you had to be somewhere in the building, but didn't have clue where that might be. They kept you off the grid, so it was a bitch finding you in this place. In fact, if it wasn't for the information Ginny gave us you'd still be strapped to that table."

I was so upset, I wasn't really listening.

All I heard was, "Ginny gave us the information we needed to find you."

"That makes no sense," I said. "Ginny, was bound and gagged. How could she have helped?"

Eric didn't answer right away. He was clearly thinking something through. Finally, the pinch in his brow relaxed a notch or two. When he finally spoke, it was with the thing he loves faking the most in life…sincerity.

"Dude, you've lost your mind," said Eric.

I have always appreciated Eric's lighthearted sense of humor, but not this time. I needed some straight answers.

"You damn near got me killed at the warehouse," I accused. "Where the hell were you?"

Judging by the change of expression, he must have realized we were talking about two different things.

"Oh, you're talking about that cluster fuck," said Eric. "Ole' George led us to the wrong warehouse. I had a bad feeling about it and shouldn't have followed the Dragons. You realize, don't you, that the West End is a wasteland of abandoned buildings?"

I knew he was right about the West End. It is a mess of a place, but Eric is a natural leader, not a follower and I couldn't understand why he would follow a ragtag group of bikers who live on the edge of the law.

"Since when do you follow anything other than your own gut?" I asked.

Eric shook his head.

"Yeah, I know," he said. "I'm sorry man. It never works out well when I ignore my instincts. Following the Dragons was a bad idea. I've been replaying the whole thing in my head. Maybe I could have kept you from catching a bullet if I'd only followed my intuition."

I could see the pain in his face. Eric blamed himself. I didn't need to keep punishing him, since he was completing that task himself. I figured I should say something to help him get through this, but I was struggling with my own shit, and besides, I didn't know what to say.

When my silence lasted long enough to make us both feel uncomfortable, Eric started talking again.

"When we finally found the right warehouse, I thought I'd find a way to flank the bad guys, but ran into one obstacle after another," said Eric.

"By the time I got to the fight, it was over."

I knew without a shadow of a doubt Eric would never miss a good fight. I was about to tell him to forget it, when he started talking again.

"The police were swarming the place and the two of you were being loaded into an ambulance," he said. "While I missed the whole damn thing, I did manage to get Uncle Jim out of that building."

"He's alive," I gasped.

"Yep and still kicking," grinned Eric. "I'm pleased to report he's as mean as ever."

"You saved Uncle Jim?" I asked.

"Well, I don't want to brag, but it was pretty damn heroic, if I do say so myself," said Eric.

"Tell me my humble friend, was he still on the roof when you found him?" I asked.

"I'm glad you have finally taken notice of my finer qualities," said Eric with a grin. "Yes, he was still on the roof. You know how he is…once a marine sniper, always a marine sniper."

"He took a high position with his rifle," I said. "It was a good plan. He can shoot the eye out of the Jack of Diamonds at ½ mile with that damn rifle, but Slotter spotted him. She's good. I don't think anyone else would have seen him. Anyway, Slotter threatened to shoot Ginny, so Uncle Jim tossed his weapon to the ground. That's pretty much when all hell broke loose."

"He wasn't alone up there," said Eric.

"Yea, I know," I said. "Pony Tail was up there too. That guy seems to be everywhere."

"It was the damnedest thing," said Eric. "I thought they were fighting at first, but now I'm not so sure."

"What did you see?" I asked.

"The smoke obscured everything," answered Eric. "But I got a glimpse of your surfer dude with Uncle Jim. At least, he sure looked an awful lot like your description of Pony Tail. At first, I thought he had Uncle Jim down and was pummeling him, but when the smoke drifted it looked more like he was helping him."

"That's weird, because I found him hovering over Ginny," I said. "At first I thought he was trying to hurt her, but now I think maybe he did something to help her."

"There's something else you need to know, Grant," said Eric. "Uncle Jim claims Pony Tail gave him medicine. He says it cured him."

"Cured him from what?" I asked.

"Everything," he answered.

Years ago, Uncle Jim fell rock climbing in the Red River Gorge. He broke his back in the fall. The doctors said he'd never walk again. Uncle Jim proved them wrong, but he uses a cane from time to time when the pain becomes too intense.

"You mean his back too?" I asked.

Eric nodded.

"That's not all," said Eric. "He swears he feels like a teenager again."

"Teenager," I said absently mindedly.

"Yea, the old goat claims the medicine has given him his mojo back," said Eric. "Geez, some players just don't know when to leave the field."

"If he's telling the truth, then that might explain why Ginny made such a miraculous recovery after I found Pony Tail hovering over her in ICU," I said.

"It seems like crazy talk to me," said Eric.

"I need to see Uncle Jim," I said. "Can you take me to him?"

"Piece of cake, Dude," said Eric. "He's down the hall negotiating your release with hospital administration."

"These people are acting like I'm their prisoner or something," I said. "Let's go see if he needs any help."

Eric led me to the patient discharge office where we found Uncle Jim glaring at a middle aged woman with scarlet colored big hair that could only have come from a bottle. Her hefty jowls were quivering like a disturbed bowl of Jell-O. I think maybe she had something important to say, but couldn't quite get it out.

Uncle Jim is a serious badass. The Marine Corps trained him for a hush-hush special ops unit that he never talks about. His job was to assassinate bad guys for Uncle Sam and I'm pretty sure he was damn good at it. Scarlet was way out of her league.

He was wearing his usual faded jeans and Harley t-shirt. To keep his fashion statement fresh and interesting, Uncle Jim likes to alternate between square toed biker boots and Jesus sandals. Today it was sandals.

Thanks to a lean muscular frame, he looks much younger than his true age. His hair is more pepper than salt, with only a touch of a receding hairline. He lost an eye in a rock climbing accident and wears a patch like a proud pirate.

He leaned in toward Scarlet and fixed his one eye on her two.

"On whose orders is he being held?" demanded Uncle Jim.

He didn't give her a chance to answer before adding, "And don't say the doctor's. There is something shady going on here and we both know it."

I imagine Scarlet was a seasoned administrator with years of experience dealing with the disgruntled public. She looked pretty damn tough to me, but she had met her match.

Uncle Jim knows how to win a fight. It

doesn't matter if it's against the Taliban or a skilled public relations expert. He is relentless and she was beginning to crack under the pressure.

"Aaawk, tell us the truth toots and we'll let you go unharmed," squawked Bird.

I was shocked to see that my foul mouth macaw was still alive. I don't know how I could have missed him standing there on Scarlet's file cabinet with his colorful feathers all in a ruffle, but I did. The last time I saw him, he went down underneath a huge man. I thought he had been squashed like a bug.

Dad had adored the bird for some strange reason. Me, well I think Bird is obnoxious and wasn't real happy when he was left to my care. Fortunately, he and Uncle Jim seem to get along pretty good, so I let my uncle take care of him most of the time. Despite our issues, I was happy to see Bird alive.

Uncle Jim has a way of dropping his chin a fraction of an inch and clenching his jaw when he doesn't approve of something. If you know what to look for, then you can see a little quiver in his jaw line just below the ear lobe. That's exactly what I saw him do in response to Bird's silly threat.

Scarlet seemed surprised by Bird's coherent speech, but it might have been too much to expect her to actually answer him. Instead she kept her eyes squarely on the bigger threat, Uncle Jim, while half-heartedly mumbling something about no pets allowed in the hospital.

Uncle Jim turned to me and winked. I nodded toward the door.

"Never mind, Uncle Jim," I said. "It doesn't matter who wants to hold him prisoner here because he's leaving with me."

Scarlet bristled, but looked relieved to see Uncle Jim turn toward the door. I doubt she knew who I was and no one else tried to stop us as we left the building. Once outside, Uncle Jim lit up like a Christmas tree.

"Grant, aren't you a sight for sore eyes," said Uncle Jim. "It's good to see you, son."

I thought I'd lost him to the flames and I'm pretty sure that explains the wave of emotion I was desperately trying to hold back. Since I couldn't seem to find my voice, I gave Uncle Jim a bear hug instead.

"Aaawk, group hug," squawked Bird as he landed gently on my shoulder and cradled us with his colorful wings.

I have never felt closer to Bird then I did in that moment.

"I'm glad you're alive," I said.

"Aaawk, thanks Peckerwood, but what about that one eyed monster horning in on our hug," squawked Bird.

"Awe, I'm gonna live forever," said Uncle Jim, "but if you keep calling me one eyed monster, then your life expectancy will be considerably shorter."

"Yea, I wanted to talk to you about that," I said. "What happened on the roof?"

"It was the damnedest thing," he said. "The building caught fire and the blaze went viral. I was trapped by the inferno and choking on the foulest black smoke I've ever encountered. My pants caught fire and burned me pretty good before I put it out."

"To make matters worse, the flames were closing in," he said. "If I didn't move quickly, then I'd never get out of there alive, except my damn legs wouldn't move. I really thought I might be a goner."

I've heard Uncle Jim tell many stories of his harrowing escapes over the years. He's like a big cat with nine lives. Somehow he always finds a way to survive. Still, we had a little tradition. When he reached the critical point in his story, he would pause, tilt his head slightly, and wait for me to ask the question.

"How did you manage to get out of that one, Uncle Jim," I asked.

He smiled a crooked smile and with a twinkle in his eye said, "The hippie helped me."

"Are you talking about the guy up on the roof with you…the one with his blond hair pulled back into a pony tail?" I asked.

"That's him," he answered.

"This guy has been popping up everywhere," I said. "What was he doing on the roof?"

"Damn if I know," answered Uncle Jim. "I didn't even know he was up there with me, until Slotter ordered us to throw our guns off the roof. I thought I moved quietly, but that guy is a ghost."

"How did he help you?" I asked.

"He gave me a pinch of herb and asked if I knew how to use snuff," he answered.

"What was it?" I asked.

"I don't know," he answered.

"Why would you put something up your nose without knowing what it was?" I asked.

Uncle Jim looked slightly embarrassed.

"I'm not sure," he said. "But maybe it was his eyes."

I was stunned. Uncle Jim was as tough and practical as they come. He isn't the type of guy who ever would say out loud that another guy's eyes affected him, let alone trust him enough to inhale an unknown substance.

It could have been the way I was looking at him, but Uncle Jim seemed eager to add, "It smelled like sunshine."

"Sunshine," I repeated incredulously.

He nodded.

"I felt a wave of intense pleasure when I inhaled it," said Uncle Jim. "It was better than sex."

"Better than sex," I repeated.

Uncle Jim winked.

"Intense pleasure," I added.

Uncle Jim giggled like a school girl. I'm pretty sure that was a first.

"Then the most amazing thing happened," said Uncle Jim.

Uncle Jim just stood there looking at me with the goofiest shit eating grin I'd ever seen on his face.

"Are you going to tell me about this amazing thing that happened next?" I asked.

I didn't think his smile could get any bigger, but it did.

"I'm glad you finally asked," he said. "It healed me."

"Healed you," I said.

He nodded. I waited for further explanation. It didn't come.

"What did it heal?" I asked.

"Everything," he said.

"Eric mentioned something about that," I said.

"The burns, my bad back…everything, except for growing back my missing eye," he said.

"Well that would be asking for a lot," I said. "It would make this whole story unbelievable, don't you think?"

"He told me there is a way to do that too, but it will have to wait until we have more time," he said.

"Grow a missing eye back," I said.

Uncle Jim nodded.

"Did he happen to tell you how that is possible?" I asked.

Uncle Jim shook his head.

"And you believe him," I said.

Uncle Jim grinned.

"Did he say when he would perform this miracle cure?" I asked.

"Nope," said Uncle Jim. "He said he had been called back to Amazonia, but would return when he could.

"Amazonia," I repeated.

Uncle Jim said, "Yep. Then he disappeared into the smoke."

"Are you telling me he vanished into thin air...like a damn ghost or something?" I asked.

Uncle Jim plastered an exaggerated hurt look on his face and said, "Somehow I don't think you believe me."

I gave Uncle Jim a long hard look, but he didn't show any signs of wavering on this, so I turned to Eric and asked, "Can you shed any light on this?"

Eric shook his head.

"I couldn't see clearly through all the smoke, but I saw Pony Tail hovering over him," said Eric. "When the smoke shifted, I lost sight of both of them for a few minutes. After it cleared again, Pony Tail was gone and Uncle Jim was walking toward me."

"I knew we didn't have much time and needed to get off the roof as fast as possible," said Uncle Jim.

"I tried to lead him out the way I had come in, but the path was blocked by flames," said Eric.

"Aaawk, these knuckleheads would be dead if it wasn't for me," said Bird.

"I thought you were squashed underneath that tank of a man," I said.

Bird held his wings like a body builder flexing cantaloupe sized biceps.

"Aaawk, with guns like these, baby, there will never be a chance anyone will squash me like a bug," said Bird.

Uncle Jim snorted, but when Bird glared at him he thought better of it and changed his attitude.

"It's true Bird guided us out of there," said Uncle Jim. "He rose above the inferno like a majestic phoenix and led us to safety."

I can't say for sure, but I think I heard Bird

purr like a kitten and bat his eyelashes. He can be impossible when his ego is allowed to run unchecked. It was time to change the subject.

"I'd have never thought that old warehouse would go up in flames so easily...or expected a Harley to explode on impact," I said. "Did the biker chick survive her last second tumble from the bike?"

"Yea, but she's pretty damn bitter about the broken hip," said Eric. "She says it's an old lady injury."

"Were any of the other Dragons injured?" I asked.

I was talking about the Dragon Gate Motorcycle Club. It was their President, Tiny, who was stabbed in the chest at the Center. They were out for revenge and tagged along on our mission to rescue Ginny.

"Ole George was shot in the ass," said Eric. "If the rest of them weren't so scared of him, they might enjoy giving him some grief over taking one in the ass. Instead, they are waiting on him hand and foot."

"Was anyone else shot?" I asked.

"Just you," said Uncle Jim.

"Was Ginny shot?" I asked.

Eric looked at me like I might be a little crazy after all and said, "You were there, Dude."

"Between the eyes," said Uncle Jim.

"Aaawk, it wasn't pretty," said Bird.

"So, I'm not crazy," I said.

Eric let out a little sigh of exasperation. Uncle Jim raised an eyebrow. It was the one over the patch. He only raised the one over the patch for seriously stupid comments.

Bird chimed in, "Aaawk, bat shit crazy if you ask me."

"When I found her in the hospital room, she was perfectly healthy," I said. "How is that possible?"

Uncle Jim and Eric gave each other a knowing look, but said nothing. They just waited, as if I was a small child that couldn't quite keep up.

"Do you think Pony Tail had anything to do with it?" I asked.

The three of them stared at me like I was retarded, but it was necessary to treat me in a politically sensitive manner. I'm not sure we've ever been politically sensitive with each other. It was weird.

"He must have used the magic herb on her," said Uncle Jim. "We need to find him."

It felt like I had fallen down Alice's rabbit hole. Uncle Jim was a tough minded old marine. Magic was not something he believed in. Somehow this hippie had gotten under his skin.

"I need to find Ginny," I said.

Eric became very interested in his shoes.

"Give it up, Grant," said Eric. "I told you. She's gone."

I was about to snap at him, but caught myself before I said something regretful. Instead, I counted two breaths. It helped immensely, since I couldn't stay mad at Eric for long. He was a good friend. If he couldn't tell me, then he had a good reason. Besides, I knew where she went and had already decided to go after her.

"Eric, I'm not sure what she said to you to get this level of loyalty, but I'm catching the first plane to Rio de Janeiro," I said. "You can come with or stay. It's your choice."

CHAPTER 4

Eric didn't ask why I thought Ginny was in Brazil. In fact, he didn't bat an eye at my plan to search for her in the Rainforest. This confirmed what I already knew, bolstered by Slotter's belief that her father is still alive, Ginny plans to search the Amazon Rainforest for him.

It bothered me that Pony Tail is also traveling to Brazil. He keeps popping up wherever Ginny happens to be and I don't like it one bit. Eric made it pretty clear Ginny was pissed at me and I feared it had something to do with Pony Tail.

I tried to convince myself that I wasn't jealous of Pony Tail, but I knew I was lying to myself. It didn't help that I had treated Ginny badly for years and knew very little about the life she had built for herself. Those thoughts just added guilt and regret to the jealous feelings I was desperately trying to deny.

Even though Uncle Jim was now Pony Tail's greatest fan, I didn't trust him. How could I trust someone who tried to kill Padma? Geez, this guy shot me. I wasn't buying this crap about him being some kind of healer. Still, there was a part of me that wanted Pony Tail to be a healer. If he really did heal Uncle Jim then I couldn't help but wonder if he couldn't work his miracles on Mom.

I needed to find this guy and get some answers. Hopefully, I could do that sooner, rather than later. The clock was ticking on Mom's eviction from Shady Days and I wasn't convinced I could sell her house in time to pay the bill and stop them from putting her out. Particularly, since my wife was threatening to get a court order to stop the sale even though Mom could die without the medical supervision they provide.

Eric accepted the offer to travel to Brazil, but not without a friendly dig or two. He patted me on the head saying I had the relationship I.Q. of a middle-schooler. On top of that, my best friend had the nerve to tell me I couldn't be left alone with a beautiful woman, like I needed a babysitter or something.

Eric knows my boundaries well enough and I was about to give him hell for crossing them when he quickly switched the discussion to Brazil's reputation for tiny bikinis. With his trademark shit eating grin, he whispered loud enough to be heard in an auditorium that Brazilian thongs are just the right size to titillate a man's imagination. I was worried about Ginny and not particularly interested in talking about bikinis, but the distraction worked well enough I didn't give him a hard time about his disrespectful behavior toward me.

There's something else that was bothering me. Ginny is afraid of me. I had seen it in her eyes twice now. The first time was when she found me in the women's bathroom cleaning blood off myself. I know it sounds awful, but I got blood all over myself when I was trying to save a man's life.

This last time was different. I know I overreacted, but I couldn't let them send back to the psyche ward. The worst part of it is I think I understand why Ginny feels this way. She suffered from years of abuse at the hand of her violent mother. I understand it because I also suffered because of her mother. I got daily shock treatments from Sadistic Doctor because of her mother. Ginny's mother had wreaked havoc in our lives, and until we stop taking it personally, the effects of her mother's abuse will continue to rob us of the life we are meant to have together.

We invited Uncle Jim to travel with us to Brazil, but he was acting mysterious and all he would say about it was he needed to follow-up on something. I was curious, but learned long ago to stay out of his private affairs. The man had his secrets and it was pointless to pry into them.

Of course, Bird was damn pissed he wasn't invited to come with us. There was no reasoning with him. Especially, when we told him he'd have to travel in a crate as cargo. He was outraged that birds couldn't fly first class, and spent considerable time grumbling about the value of diversity.

Eventually he gave up his bitching, but not before saying, "Aaawk, why the hell would I want to get on a damn airplane anyway. I got my own wings, baby."

"Yes you do," I agreed.

To reinforce our sensitivity to his plight, we nodded in unison. It's best to not piss Bird off too much. He relaxed a notch or two, so it was working, but to make certain we got the point he flexed his biceps body builder style and added a final comment.

"Aaawk, this bird is a bad ass in the air!"

There wasn't much response to that except for a snarky comeback or two that came to mind, but I sure wasn't willing to set him off again and since Bird was in no mood for a ribbing, I focused instead on getting us tickets. I used the latest travel app on my phone to make the purchase.

There was a tense moment when the app took its sweet time spitting out a flight confirmation. I was sure it was going to report my credit card had been summarily rejected thanks to my wife's spending problems. However, it was eventually approved and after hastily packing a carryon bag, we rushed to the airport.

People stared as we boarded the plane for Rio de Janeiro. Maybe I was a little self-conscious, but I hadn't showered or shaved for days and had to fight the temptation to sniff my pits. I only won that battle because I figured it would just draw more attention to us.

I had to shake my head and grin at Eric as he bounded to our seats and claimed the window. I wanted that window seat, but yielded it to him as gracefully as I could. I had more important things on my mind and he was my best friend, after all.

We managed to settle into our seats without anyone sniffing the air distastefully or demanding to be moved to a new seat. There was a long flight ahead of us and for the first time, I allowed myself to consider the daunting task ahead, but before I descended too far into despair, Eric jolted me back with an elbow to my sore ribs.

Leaning over us was a flight attendant with close cropped brown hair, big boobs, and a touch of light pink lipstick. Her green eyes were filled with warmth and I sensed she was quick to see the humor in ordinary things.

"Sir, you have the seat next to the emergency

exit," she said.

I cut my eyes to the emergency door and nodded.

She leaned in a little closer and dropped her voice an octave, "In the unlikely event of an emergency can you open that door and assist the other passengers off the plane."

I nodded once again.

She squeezed my bicep and said, "Whatever you're worrying about will work out for the best."

Before I could thank her, she winked and sashayed off.

Eric elbowed me yet again and said, "There you go, Dude, words of wisdom from the in-flight nurse."

I raised an eyebrow, but said nothing.

"Geez you're so damn uptight," said Eric with a sigh. "The Tao keeps throwing beautiful women at you, 'cuz it knows what you need. You just gotta learn to relax and flow with it."

He's right about the women. They're always throwing themselves at me. I don't think they do it because I'm more attractive than the next guy. Instead, I think they sense I'm not interested in casual hook-ups.

It's like they have a radar for men like me who hunger for happily ever after. All I ever wanted was to be loved, and since they want the same thing, it draws them to me like flies to cow patties.

Eric was waiting for a response, so I said, "I'm here to help Ginny, not hook-up with a flight attendant."

He shook his head and said, "A fool on a fool's mission, my friend."

"Speaking of missions, have you had any luck finding Ch'ing?" I asked.

Eric shook his head.

I didn't press him for details. We were both upset by the disappearance of our martial arts teacher a few days earlier. It was very odd since Ch'ing never went anywhere. He was always there for us and when he didn't' show up at the dojo for class, Eric sent someone to investigate. Much to our dismay, Ch'ing's front door was standing open and his home was trashed leading us to fear the worst.

Eric turned toward the window and acted like he was settling in for a nap, but I think he just wanted to hide his tears.

I let him be and returned to my worries. How the hell am I going to find Ginny in the vastness of the Amazon Rainforest? I'm generally an optimist, but was beginning to think this was a seriously ill-conceived venture. Maybe Eric is right. I'm on a fool's mission.

Overwhelmed with a growing sense of

impending doom, I searched on my smartphone for Ginny's company, Emerald Allure, to see what I could learn. I knew she had a factory somewhere in Brazil and I figured that would be her base of operations while she searched the rainforest for her father.

A few days earlier, Ginny had told me the story of how she got her start in the clothing business. Like many things in life, it was happenstance, but she had the vision to build it into one of the world's fastest growing companies.

The thing I admire most about her is the commitment to building a company with heart. While other companies exploit the poor, she finds ways to empower her employees.

Earlier, I had downloaded information about Brazil from the State Department's website. The thing that struck me the hardest was the country's involvement in the slave trade. It was a disheartening read about the many ways the desperate are exploited.

For example, unethical companies use bonded labor to clear trees in the Rainforest. The trees are used to manufacture charcoal for barbeque grills in the United States. The Rainforest is home to a wide diversity of plant and animal life. Once stripped of plant life, the naked land offers the creatures little refuge.

These companies go into the slums of Rio de Janeiro and promise the desperately poor a better life. Instead of a life-upgrade, they get long hours, unsafe conditions, and little or no pay. The slavers think nothing of exploiting the poor's only possession, their hope.

The recruits acquire debts for travel and living expense that they never pay off. They are prisoners of a lie and the vast jungle serves as their prison bars.

After reading about the charcoal industry, I vowed to never use it again. Not that I owned a grill or even a backyard for that matter, but it was the principle of the thing.

Ginny's company is different. Emerald Allure hires the poor, gives them good pay, health benefits and safe working conditions. It is more like collaboration than a traditional employment relationship. It may be a drop in the bucket, but she is trying her best to make a change.

While I admire her commitment to change, I'm not sure what to think about this obsessive search for her father after twenty years in the jungle. Even if it were true, which I seriously doubt, the Amazon Rainforest is vast…over two million square miles. I wonder how she expects to find him in all of that wilderness.

Stranger still, both Slotter and Mr. Suit are looking for her father as well. I don't know what they want with him, but they are willing to use violence. Ginny is in grave danger. I need to find her fast and it isn't going to be easy.

I also need to find Pony Tail. This business about him curing Uncle Jim and Ginny seems incredible to me, but I want to keep an open mind because Mom needs help.

A wave of hopelessness tried to push its way into my mind, but I pushed back. This is not the time to give in to despair. Somehow, I will find Pony Tail and learn more about this medicine, but first I need to complete my mission and find Ginny. Failure is not an option.

With a sigh, I decided to get some rest. As my eyelids closed, I opened the door to the inner eye and pictured Ch'ing standing before us. He's short, a pinch shy of 5'4", and can't weigh more than a buck twenty soaking wet. His size and coloring suggests he is originally from Southeast Asia, but since he deflects all questions about his origins, no one knows for sure where he actually came from.

Ch'ing wears his black hair in a long braid that hangs below the shoulder blades. Sparse whiskers and smooth skin make him look more like a teenager than a grown man. I sometimes think of him as an older brother, until I look into his ancient eyes and see a man who knows eternity as well as you might know your favorite television show. Ch'ing is timeless.

"Well, what do you two hooligans know about gathering energy?" he once asked.

I looked at Eric for an answer, but his blank face told me that he was just as clueless as me about Ch'ing's question. At the time, we were no older than ten and I'm pretty sure that we had an overabundance of energy. At least that's what the nuns at catholic school told us.

"Aaawk, it won't do you any good to try sandbagging us, because we have ways to make you talk," squawked Bird.

Bird's favorite torture is to drag his claws across a pane of glass. When we were kids, the screeching sent our hands to ears, followed by rounds of belly-laughs. The funny thing is, it really works, because after the laughter died down, we would spout whatever came to mind just to get him to stop and Ch'ing almost always approved of these spontaneous answers.

"I always feel full of energy after school," I said.

"Good!" said Ch'ing. "Why do you think that is?"

"I don't know, maybe it's because I'm happy to be free again," I answered.

"That's right!" said Ch'ing. "When someone forces us to do something we don't want to do, it causes tension, and tension robs us of our Chi."

"What's tension?" asked Eric.

"Awe, very good question Master Eric," said Ch'ing.

We always liked it when Ch'ing called us Master. It made us feel grown-up and important.

"For example, the way you boys just puffed your chest out is good tension, " said Ch'ing.

"Is there bad tension?" asked Eric.

"I'm glad you asked," said Ch'ing. "You are such an intelligent young man."

He rubbed his eight chin whiskers and looked up toward the left. Ch'ing always did that when he was thinking up an exercise for us. Some of those exercises were fun, but others we didn't like too much.

"I know you boys don't want a lecture from me, so let's give you a way to experience tension firsthand," said Ch'ing.

We might have groaned just a little.

"I'm glad you two agree," he said with a twinkle in his eye. "Here's what I want you to do. Hold your hands about chest high, palms facing downward."

As always, he demonstrated exactly what he expected us to do. We looked at each other, shrugged, and did as instructed.

"Well done!" said Ch'ing. "How did I get so lucky as to have the Tao send me two brilliant young students?"

We suspected he was pulling our legs, but praise from Ch'ing wasn't something we ever took lightly.

"Now, take a deep breath and squeeze your fists, as hard, and as long as you can," said Ch'ing. "Come on boys. No slacking. Really squeeze hard."

As usual, Eric and I made a competition of it, determined to hold it longer than the other. It's harder than it looks. We were both sweating in a matter of minutes and soon quit.

"I beat you," said Eric.

"No, I beat you," I said.

"Aaawk, nobody wins," said Bird. "It's a tie and ties are lame."

Ch'ing was smiling as he smoothed out his skimpy mustache.

"Why did you give up so easily?" he asked.

"It's hard," I grumbled.

"Yeah, it's way harder than it looks," said Eric.

"That squeezing is one example of tension," said Ch'ing. "It's hard because it drains us of energy really fast. It is a waste of energy and Taoist like us don't like to waste energy.

"You mean we shouldn't squeeze so hard," I asked.

"I mean, the first lesson of Chi Kung is to stop wasting energy," said Ch'ing.

"How do we do that?" asked Eric.

"You begin by relaxing any muscles, including your noggin, that aren't required for the task at hand," said Ch'ing.

I'm pretty sure all Ch'ing saw was two boys with blank faces, because he looked us up and down and then shook his head with exaggerated sadness.

"Think of it like a cat," said Ch'ing. "They lay around sleeping all day, but as soon as that mouse tries to sneak out and steal a meal, the cat pounces."

To add emphasis, he snapped his fingers just when the cat pounces.

"Relax and gather energy," said Ch'ing. "When you spring into action, do it completely and without hesitation. Act without tension, because tension slows you down and divides you against yourself."

The Captain interrupted the trip into the past with a message about turbulence and seat belts. Eric stirred, but his eyes never opened. Instead, he went back to snoring softly with the left side of his face smashed against the window.

I closed my eyes again and rested for a few minutes. Gradually, my breathing deepened until it reached the soles of my feet. Breath carries oxygen to every cell of our bodies. It exchanges nutrients for waste products and then eliminates them with every exhalation. It was comforting to know that my breath does this without any effort on my part.

When it was time, I slowly and methodically searched for tension. It wasn't hard to find. There was a lot of tension in my body. Wherever I found it, I replaced it with a smile. My inner smile slowly worked its magic dissolving tension and replacing it with contentment. It was going to be a long flight. I was in no hurry and permitted myself to sink deeper into a delicious, relaxed state.

I must have fallen asleep, because I woke from a dream filled nap as the plane began its final descent into Rio. The view was spectacular. Sugar Loaf Mountain stood at the gateway to the city like a rounded pyramid that had seen better days. Then there was the iconic statute of Christ welcoming travelers to the city with open arms.

They say the statute is one of the Seven Wonders of the World, but for me it was just a reminder of too many hours spent attending long boring Masses. In addition to Sunday services, we began school each morning with church. That left only Saturday mornings to rest my weary spirit from the somber ritual.

Unfortunately, when I served as an altar boy I always seemed to get assigned to Saturday morning Mass. Seven days a week is way too much religion for anybody, especially a kid who spends church service plotting his escape. I wanted to run barefoot in the grass, not kneel at the foot of the altar.

Galeão International Airport came into view below. I wondered what the architect had in mind when he designed it as circle split into halves. It seemed to symbolize division.

In contrast, I remembered an image from a weird dream I had just before I woke. I was in an eight sided chamber lined with stone. In the center of the room was a pool of water. "Water's Edge" was written above the pool in an ancient script. In sharp contrast to the fragmented life I was struggling to put back together, the chamber filled me with a soothing sense of wholeness

Padma was in my dream and I asked him, "What is Water's Edge?"

"There is an ancient pool of water deep in the jungle," he answered. "Many years ago a temple was built around it. We call this place Water's Edge."

"Why would anyone build a temple around a pool of water?" I asked.

Padma's eyes glistened as he answered, "It is the water of life. From this pool springs eternal life."

"You can't be serious," I said. "Are you telling me this is the mythical Fountain of Youth?"

"Open your mind," said Padma.

I figured I was more open-minded than the next guy and was about to argue the point when the plane touched down and rattled me out of the dream.

As we to a stop I remembered something Ch'ing once said about immortality. All of eternity is contained in the present moment. The past and the future are illusions. Living in the past is a sickness because it was never really the way we remember. Hurrying headlong from the present moment into an uncertain future is likewise an illness to be avoided at all costs. Immortality is living your life fully in the present and in such a manner that others want you to live forever.

Whenever we found ourselves surrounded by people in a rush, Ch'ing encouraged us to slow down and pay attention to everything around us. As usual, he had an exercise to demonstrate his point.

Holding our arms out to the side, he had us spin clockwise until the world around us became a blur. This blur is what people experience when they rush about. In their haste, they fail to focus on the thing right in front of them. They ignore the reality at their feet. Ch'ing called it a state of ignorance. He encouraged us to find our center and become the eye in the middle of the storm that sees clearly.

Because of this conditioning, Eric and I were able to wait patiently as our fellow passengers rushed to escape the flying tin can. Once the others were off the plane, we made our way into the airport terminal. I was surprised that it was a modern facility. For some reason, I had expected it to be more primitive…more third world.

Everyone else moved as a herd toward baggage claim. Since Eric and I hadn't checked our bags, we split from the crowd and made our way to ground transportation where we found a crowd of travelers milling around. There wasn't a single bus or taxi within sight and the restless crowd was growing by the minute.

Eric and I had been friends long enough that sometimes we behave like an old married couple. There isn't any need for forced conversation between us. If we have something to say, we say it. Otherwise, we keep to our thoughts. This was one of our quiet moments.

My thoughts were interrupted by an unknown caller on my cell phone. Thanks to a growing stack of bills at home, I usually ignored these calls, but my gut told me this one was important and so I reluctantly took it.

"This is Grant Li," I said.

"Is this Grant Li?" asked a woman.

I resisted the temptation to snap at her for not listening and instead answered politely, "Yes, it is.

Who is this?"

She ignored my question and stuck to her script.

"Mr. Li, I am calling on behalf of the Shady Days Adult Care Center," she said.

My mother has been a resident at Shady Days facility since the motorcycle crash that left her a quadriplegic and killed my father twenty years earlier. Recently, she took a turn for the worse after a bad drug reaction.

To make matters worse, they are evicting her at the end of the month. Since the doctor has to put her on life support from time to time, this turn of events has put her life at risk.

"Is my mother okay?" I asked.

"Mr. Li, we are calling to tell you that the insurance company has denied your claim," she said.

The insurance ran out years ago, so I knew for sure she was reading from a script.

"Can you please tell me whether my mother is okay?" I said.

"Mr. Li, we have you down as the responsible party," said Ms. Nobody.

I finally snapped at her.

"Does my mother need anything?" I shouted.

"Mr. Li, the balance on the account is $332,456.22," she said. "I can take your credit card information now. Do you have it ready?"

I was stunned.

"Mr. Li, what is your card number?" she asked.

I hung up on her. Between the ravages of divorce and losing my job, I was broke. I had no idea what I was going to do. I just knew I had to do something and do it soon.

"Breathe," said Eric.

My friend was staring intently into my eyes. He didn't know what was happening, but he knew the call upset me. I needed help and he was there for me. Eric was pulling me back into the present.

"Bill collector," I said as if that explained it all.

"Just take a deep breath," he said.

That was as good a place as any to start, so I gulped down a big bite of air. Once I let that one out, I took another, and then another, until finally, I settled back into the present moment.

"What just happened?" asked Eric.

"I'm in trouble," I said.

"I know," he said. "But you don't have to face it alone."

Eric and I had been friends for a long time, but there were parts of my life that I didn't share with him. I always figured a man doesn't burden others with personal matters. These things must be faced alone. Maybe that's a mistake. Maybe it's time to open my life.

I was about to unburden myself when a lone

bus rolled in and came to a stop in front of us. Even though we didn't have a clue where it was headed, it was the only option available to us, so we climbed aboard.

The crowd squeezed in and when the bus couldn't possibly hold another body, the driver shut the door and pulled away. I was afforded a view out a small slice of a window and gratefully took it since the next best option was to stare down the huge backside of a woman with a 1960's style beehive hairdo.

I absent-mindedly gazed out the window of the bus and was shocked to see Ginny displayed on a giant digital billboard. She held the rainforest in her arms like a mother holding a newborn child for the first time. Her eyes were filled with the wonder of precious new life.

I have to confess she looked like the Madonna holding baby Jesus, but it didn't make me feel a bit better. Instead, I thought of my own mother lying wasted in a hospital bed desperate for a cure.

The last good memory of my mother was the morning of the motorcycle crash. It was my dad's birthday and we were together for the last time. Mom's gift to my dad was the Harley he always dreamed of owning. After dropping me off at school, my parents took the Harley out for a maiden ride. I never saw my father again thanks to a hit and run driver.

Mom survived the crash, but is a quadriplegic. The doctors tried to strip away our hope by telling us there is no cure and the best we can do is make her last few months comfortable. That was twenty years ago, but I've never given up hope that they would someday find a way to heal her broken body.

My rumination about Mom was interrupted when the bus suddenly swerved to the right squeezing me between Eric and the Beehive. An explosion sent glass flying everywhere. The scent of burning rubber was followed by a crash that jerked us forward. It slammed my forehead hard enough into the back of the forward seat that I saw stars.

My head was pounding, or at least that's what I thought at first. I was trying to shake off the effects of the blow, when I saw hands pounding on the window. The bus was surrounded by an angry mob.

"Grant, we need to get out of here," said Eric.

I nodded in agreement. The bus was beginning to feel like a death trap. The other passengers were still in shock, but some were beginning to stir. I feared they would soon panic and wanted out before they stampeded the doors. Squeezing out of my seat, I began elbowing a path to the door.

We were nearly to the front of the bus when a man sprung from his seat and drove a shoulder into my already sore ribs. They had taken a beating over the last few days and I was determined to protect them at all costs. I instinctively slammed a knee into his face and watched him crumble to the floor.

Eric nodded toward the door and said something to the bus driver in Portuguese. The driver responded by pointing to a 70's model car burning in the street and shook his head.

A line of helmeted police rushed to the fire where they clashed with unarmed men. A police baton ripped open a teenager's face from the corner of his eye to his ear lobe. The poor guy staggered too close to the fire and the flame ignited his shirt. Panicked, he ran in the general direction of the bus.

"Oh hell no," I shouted as I drove my foot through the door.

A woman running past the bus toward the burning kid was caught by the door and knocked to the ground. Pain shot through my ribs as I jumped over her crumbled body.

Eric followed me out of the bus and squatted next to her. He gently placed his hands on a wound oozing blood from the back of her head. Her eyes flickered open and she murmured something to him. After exchanging a few words, he helped her to her feet.

Concerned I asked, "Is the wound serious?"

"The cut will heal," answered Eric. "Her wounded mind is more serious. She told me a group of policeman assaulted her daughter. The authorities denied it. The police said the girl was working for a local drug dealer and they were only trying to get information from her."

Eric waived his arm toward the angry mob.

"These people are upset, so they took to the streets in peaceful protest of police corruption," said Eric. "Things got out of control when the police used tear gas and the demonstration quickly turned into a riot."

The woman was mumbling something to herself as she picked at an imaginary wound on her forearm. She seemed lost to herself. I couldn't imagine the pain she felt. A stone whizzed past my head and smashed into the side of the bus.

"Speaking of the riot, we better get out of here," I said.

Eric led me into a shantytown filled with poorly constructed buildings pieced together from scraps of wood, cinder block and chicken wire.

"What is this place?" I asked.

"Favela," he answered.

"Huh?" Was my brilliant response.

"It's a Brazilian ghetto," said Eric.

"I was under the impression Rio is a rich modern city," I said.

"Like most places in the world it's sharply divided between rich and poor," said Eric. "In this land, there are very few in the middle."

"Where did all of these poor people come from?" I asked.

Eric shrugged.

"Many here are native people who lost their ancestral homes in the rainforest to logging and mining interests," he said.

As we circled around the crowd, Eric's phone chimed.

"I'm not sure what to make of this, but you're not going to like it," said Eric.

"The last few days have been hell for me," I said. "I was served with a petition for dissolution of marriage, lost my job, saw two people die horrible deaths, got shot…twice, watched Ginny get shot, and was nearly locked up in the loony bin. On top of all of that, they want to throw Mom out of the nursing home. I'm guessing whatever you have, will be more of the same."

Eric shook his head.

"Geez Dude, when you put that way, it sounds kind of like you've hit a rough spell," he said.

I gave him my best glare and asked, "What's up?"

"We found out who was behind your gig at the Center," he said.

Shortly after my employment was terminated from the law firm, an unknown person hired me as a bodyguard for a famous monk who was speaking at the Center. Things didn't go well. A security guard was murdered, I was shot, and thirty two hundred people in the audience died.

I figured whoever hired me was behind this nightmare and said a little impatiently, "So are you going to tell me, or what."

"It was Ginny," he said.

"Ginny?" I asked.

"Well...more precisely, it was her company, Emerald Allure," he said.

"A company that designs upscale clothing for women hired me to guard a monk in Louisville on a speaking engagement," I said.

Eric nodded.

"Was it Ginny personally?" I asked.

He shook his head.

"No, it was Victor Branco, her head of security," he said.

"It's time you tell me where Ginny is," I demanded.

"She's in Brazil," he said. "Your instincts were right, but she's not here in Rio. She's in Manaus at the gateway to the Amazon Rainforest."

"Why the hell didn't you tell me that sooner?"

I asked.

"Because Ginny asked me not to and because I wanted to do a little partying in Rio, maybe add a few bikinis to my collection," said Eric.

"Your collection," I said.

"Seriously dude, you don't think I wear them, do you?" asked Eric.

I shrugged my shoulders.

"Beats me," I said.

Eric gave me his best hurt look. He even stuck his lower lip out to add a little pout to enhance the overall affect.

"Where is Victor Branco?" I asked.

"Manaus," answered Eric.

"Then we need to get to Manaus," I said.

"Yep."

CHAPTER 5

In sharp contrast to the lack of transportation at the Rio airport, there was a string of eager taxi drivers hustling to make a buck at the Manaus terminal. They were backed into parking slots with the trunk lids open, urging us with a wave to load our bags into their vehicle. None seemed to notice we carried no luggage.

A pear shaped guy leaped with surprising agility from a three wheeler hugging the curb in a no parking zone and huffed in our direction. The other drivers were wearing white short-sleeve shirts and tan slacks, but this guy stood out in pink polyester yoga pants stretched to the max across his broad ass and a canary yellow t-shirt that sagged in all the wrong places. He had a likeable round face, large mouth and tiny white teeth.

"Hello, my friends, I am Paulo," he said. "Welcome to Amazonia."

His cab was part motor scooter and part car. It was barely wide enough in the front to support Paulo's ample derriere, but could easily seat two in the rear. It was white with a black convertible top that provided shade from the equatorial sun.

Paulo must have seen the doubt on my face because he said, "Not to worry my friends. I have the best rates in Manaus thanks to the vastly superior gas mileage I get from this most amazing and very safe machine."

Eric poked me in the ribs and said, "Come on, Dude, live on the edge for a change."

I shrugged and we climbed into the back of the cab. The inside had the same hard plastic seats you'd find in a golf cart, but Paulo had softened them for his customers with colorful hand sewn cushions. A small wind chime, hand crafted into the shapes of endangered jungle critters, dangled from the rear view mirror. It provided musical accompaniment to Paulo's incessant chattering about Manaus.

"Where to my friends?" asked Paulo.

"Emerald Allure," I said.

"Are you rich Americans here to shop in the free trade zone?" he asked.

I shook my head.

"Yes, we go to the free trade zone," said Paulo answering his own question. "Scenic route today, my friends?"

"No," I answered.

"Yes, I want to see the real Manaus," said Eric.

"Very good choice, my friend, we take the scenic route and I show rich American shoppers the real Manaus," said Paulo.

The road leading out of the airport cut through green space dotted with occasional industrial buildings. There were patches of wind farms adjacent to the factories where huge blades reminiscent of airplane propellers spun atop a single mast to generate an alternative source of energy.

It was in the low nineties and humid. A bank of clouds riding the southeast trade winds rolled in from the east, serving as a reminder that this city had been carved out of the jungle and it's true nature is wet and primitive.

"Did you know, my friends, that Manaus is named after the Mother of the Gods?" asked Paulo.

I pulled my eyes from the roadside scenery and met his gaze in the rear view mirror. He didn't expect or wait for an answer. Paulo is one of those people who just like to talk.

"This beautiful city was once considered the Paris of the Tropics," he said. "You been there…to Paris, France?"

I shook my head.

"Well, this is a city of romance," he said. "We have many pretty people who live here."

So far, I had only met Paulo and he wasn't my type.

The cab turned down an umbrella lined street

filled with shops, restaurants and open markets displaying colorful fruits and vegetables. Two small girls, about seven years old, squatted next to an anaconda that was thicker by far than their skinny legs. One controlled the head while the other pinned the tail to the ground. A scruffy medium sized dog with shaggy black hair squatted nearby with a bored expression on his face.

These four story buildings were old, but most were well-maintained. They were painted with bright tropical pinks, yellows, and lime greens. The food smelled amazing and my stomach growled in appreciation.

"We have festivals in Manaus…many festivals," he said. "We love to fiesta, and you my friends, have arrived just in time to enjoy the boat parade."

Paulo made several more turns before pulling to a stop in front of a modern six story building displaying a bold sign that announced, "Welcome to Emerald City." He left the taxi running and followed us inside the building while chattering something about wanting to say hello to his cousin.

The revolving door cast us into an open area with hardwood floors softened by an occasional area rug. The colorful artwork was framed in the same distressed wood as the flooring and molding. Organic is the word that best describes the gateway to Ginny's offices.

A dark haired receptionist sat at a small table that looked like it was better suited for a coffee shop. Still, it somehow fit the space perfectly.

Her white blouse was unbuttoned far enough to reveal a deep cleavage that led my eyes downward. Once they started down that slippery slope, I couldn't seem to stop them. Just below the table top was a bit of olive green fabric that qualified as a mini-skirt.

Further down were bare legs crossed at the shins. She had at least five inches of spiked heels as a base. Her thighs opened just enough that I could see she was freshly waxed, before chastely closing again as she rose from her chair.

Paulo's huge backside moved into my field of vision as he wrapped his arms around the receptionist and gave her a platonic hug. When she broke the hug he spoke to her in rapid Portuguese before introducing her as his cousin, Aida, and us as his new best friends from Kentucky, USA.

Aida quickly scanned our left hands, taking note of Eric's wedding band. The disappointment in her eyes was clearly evident. Her predatory gaze shifted to my empty hand. Once she determined I was available, she moved in for the kill.

"Well aren't you just a hunk," she said to me in perfect English.

Thinking I might capitalize on the flirt, I flashed my best engaging smile.

"We are friends of Virginia Bardough and would like to speak with her for a few minutes, if she's available," I said.

Her eyes traveled down to my jeans, where they paused a beat.

"Sorry gorgeous, but she's not here," said Aida.

"Are you expecting her anytime soon?" I asked.

Aida shook her head and then said suggestively, "Maybe someone else can help you."

I ignored her invitation and asked, "Ginny's here in Manaus, isn't she?"

Aida froze for just an instant, and then did a bobble headed dance between a shake and a nod. Her conflicted body language left me confused and uncertain about what to do next.

Eric spoke up and asked the obvious question, "Is Victor Branco available?"

A touch of fear briefly flashed across Aida's face. Before she could formulate an answer to Eric's question, her phone buzzed. I could see a slight tremor in her hand as she reached for the handset.

Aida took a small breath to bolster herself, but her greeting was stifled before it ever got started. Instead she listened attentively to the voice on the other end. It was loud enough that I could hear it, but not loud enough to make out the words. There's one thing I can say for sure, it was a man's voice and it was demanding.

"Yes sir, I will tell them," said Aida.

She lowered the handset into the cradle like it was something she feared breaking, but really wanted to smash into a thousand pieces. When she returned her attention to me, it was different. It reminded me of the way someone looks at a sick patient they are visiting in a hospital.

"Mr. Branco can meet with you in the morning," she said. "In the meantime, relax and enjoy our festival. The Procissao Fluvial de Sao Pedro is one of my favorites. It's like your Macy's Thanksgiving Day Parade, but on water."

She dropped her voice an octave and added, "Look for me."

We thanked her and had turned to leave when I saw a door behind Aida open a few inches. An eye peeped out at us for the briefest moment and then the door silently closed once again.

As soon as we stepped outside of the building, Paulo turned to us and said, "Victor Franco is a very bad man…very bad indeed, my friends. Be careful with that one."

"Why do you say that?" I asked.

He opened his mouth to speak and then shut it again. Instead, he cut his eyes toward one of the windows above us, gave a little shutter, and then shook his head.

"Hurry, let's get you inside of my limousine," he said.

Eric jabbed me in the ribs with an elbow, but didn't need to say more. The laughter in his eyes said it all as we climbed into Paulo's limo.

"Where to next my friends…are we ready to do that shopping now?" asked Paulo.

"No shopping," said Eric.

"Can you recommend a hotel near the water?" I asked.

"Only the very finest for my rich American friends," said Paulo.

"No, something more modest," I said.

"We want a place that is clean, but with historical character," said Eric.

"I have the perfect hotel for you," said Paulo. "My cousin will make sure you get the finest and most spacious room overlooking the water."

Paulo caught my eye in the rearview mirror and winked.

"Rooms…we will need two," I said.

"As you wish," he said.

Paulo drove us past the big resorts that looked like they had been cloned from the same template used by developers all around the world. Sitting off alone at water's edge was a historic three story Spanish colonial with a gold dome and high arched windows. The stucco was painted a discreet sandstone and trimmed in white. A monkey hung from the second story balcony screaming obscenities at us between bites of a juicy mango he possessively clutched with his right foot. It was the perfect hotel for us.

After we checked into our rooms, I walked down to the beach to watch the boats parade along the river. Eric decided to skip the parade in lieu of a nap.

I spotted an empty lounge chair by the water and settled in with a fruity drink made of acai berries and rum. It was served up in a hurricane glass with a wedge of lime and the choice of a straw or a long handled pink spoon. The drink was thick and slushy enough I decided to use the spoon instead of the straw.

The boats came in all sizes and shapes. Some were decorated like floats, but others were not. More than a few were good sized party boats loaded on two levels with passengers dancing to live salsa music. Even the river dolphins enjoyed the party. Their lively antics seemed to follow the sexy Latin beat.

Between the alcohol and the events of the last few days, I began to drift off. The last boat I saw before I closed my eyes carried a large banner with a white skull sporting large orange eyes, black nose and a mouth full of horse teeth.

I'm not sure how long I slept, but it was the shrill voice of Dad's macaw that woke me.

"Aaawk, wake up peckerwood," said Bird. "You have a date with destiny."

It must have been a dream because the foul mouth bird was nowhere in sight. The sun had set and twilight fell across the empty river. A band played to a fiesta somewhere off in the distant night. The party had moved to the streets.

My stomach rumbled for food. I decided to forego hotel fare and headed instead into the thick of things in search of a place to eat with local character. The savory aroma of street food pulled me into the older part of the city.

People were dancing in the streets, each dressed in a uniquely bizarre costume lending a Mardi Gras atmosphere to the place. As I weaved through the crowd of drunks, I saw a young girl with vacant eyes and a sad demeanor standing in the center of an alley.

Despite the heat, she wore a hooded cloak that covered everything except her hands, feet and face. Those areas were covered with white powder accented by streaks of red, like smeared blood. It gave her a creepy voodoo look.

Just as I was about to turn away, Voodoo Girl collapsed. Without giving it a second thought, I rushed toward her, but a police officer stepped from the shadows and blocked my path. I froze in my tracks.

He was covered from head to toe in navy blue swat clothing. Swat Cop wore a riot helmet, dark glasses, and the remainder of his face was covered with a mask. I'm pretty sure he was wearing body armor as well. The outfit looked unbearably hot to me, but I didn't see any signs of perspiration on him.

I expected Swat Cop to do something to help Voodoo Girl, but he ignored her and instead raised his weapon and pointed it in my face. For the first time, I wondered whether he was a real cop or not. I didn't see any identifying markings for the Manaus Police Department and he seemed undisciplined to me...more like a common crook than a well-trained policeman.

As I wondered whether this might just be a mugging, a young woman wearing a wife beater and faded blue jeans appeared from the shadows. There was a snake tattooed around her right bicep. Wife Beater seemed to look right through me. I don't think I saw her blink once and was beginning to think she might be blind, but then she cut his eyes to Swat Cop and spoke.

"Bring him," said Wife Beater.

Criminals are just people who are too lazy to work. So, when they commit a crime, they want it to be easy. They do not want the crime to be anything like work and they certainly don't want to get caught.

If the crime begins at a location where there might be witnesses, one of the first things a criminal tries to do is convince the victim to go with them to a more remote location. Once they isolate the victim, then the criminal can do anything they want without worrying about getting caught. Never leave a public place and go with a criminal to a more isolated location.

I raised my hands in the air and said, "Hey, you can have my money, but I'm not going anywhere with you."

Swat Cop jammed the gun in my belly and Wife Beater asked, "Do you hear those fireworks?"

I nodded.

"No one will notice if he pulls the trigger," said Wife Beater. "The gun shot will blend in with the sounds of the fireworks. You'll just be another dead asshole on the streets of Manaus. Do you understand?"

I let out a deflated sigh and murmured, "Not good."

"Understand?" asked Wife Beater more forcefully.

I nodded.

Swat Cop spun me around and pushed hard into my mid-back with the barrel of his gun. I took the first step toward crime scene number two.

As if on cue, Voodoo Girl popped up and joined the group. It was now clear that her sudden collapse had been a ruse to lure me into their trap, but I had no idea what they wanted with me.

We made our way down to the Amazon where they had a small boat tied to the tangled roots of an uprooted tree that had washed ashore with the rest of the driftwood. Wife Beater reached behind herself and produced a coil of rough rope made from a stiff natural fiber. She handed it to Swat Cop who tightly bound my hands. When I tested the knots, I was rewarded with tortuous pain from the prickly fibers ripping into my skin.

Voodoo Girl leaned ever so slightly in my direction and sniffed as a drop of blood fell to the river bank. Her dark hunger sent a chill up my spine. It only lasted a moment before she once again became a blank page empty of human emotion. The thought of her drinking blood like a real life vampire feeding off unsuspecting tourists gave me the creeps.

Swat Cop said something to me in an unfamiliar language. I answered in English, telling him I didn't understand him. The fake policeman pointed his gun at me. I calmly stood my ground. Swat Cop snarled and pressed the barrel against my temple. I remained silent.

The cop waited and then pulled the hammer back. I felt sweat trickle down to the small of my back. Oddly, his hand trembled. I also noticed his breath wheezed, heavy and labored.

I could smell fear, but wasn't sure if it was mine or if it was his. The tremble seemed to piss him off and he pressed the cold steel deeper into my flesh. I figured I was as good as dead. There was nothing to do but wait.

My senses heightened. I swear I felt the river's life force. It seemed I was part of something bigger...a force of life that permeates all things. It reminded me of music I heard long ago. A piece from Mozart, I think, but I couldn't quite place it.

Finally, Wife Beater said something in the same strange language. Swat Cop grunted and lowered the hammer. With a small wave of the barrel, he pointed in the direction of the boat and I climbed in. I shook my head. I did not have time for this shit.

As the others climbed aboard, I felt something moving against my leg. I casually slapped at it, expecting an insect. Something hissed at me. I peered into the darkness. There was something there, but I couldn't quite make it out until the moon passed through the clouds and a beam of light revealed a huge snake.

Instinctively I sprang backward and fell over the side of the boat and into the river. Disoriented in the dark water, I struggled to find my footing and slipped under the surface a second time.

A strong hand grabbed me by the collar and yanked me back into the boat. Wife Beater's face was inches from mine. I held my breath to avoid the foul stench of her breath. It reminded me of a burnt match...full of sulfur. She scowled for a moment before allowing herself a small smile.

I nervously glanced in the snake's direction. The anaconda's lidless eyes stared back...its forked tongue flickering in and out. I suppressed a childish urge to stick mine out as well. I could be mistaken, but I'm pretty sure I saw the damn thing smirk.

Swat Cop took the helm, gunned the engine and launched us toward the center of the Amazon where black water meets brown water, but the two refuse to mix. We steered past a group of fishing boats lit up with lanterns. The fisherman used the light to sort through the days catch. As best I could tell, the river had generously provided a rich bounty, but there was something gut wrenching about seeing the fish gasp for their last breath.

Once we moved away from their lights, everything was black…the sky, the water and my mood. These people were taking me away from Manaus. To where and for what, I didn't know.

The boat ride went on for what seemed like hours. The river was crowded with drifting trees and plants we maneuvered around. I couldn't quite figure out why they were still green until I saw huge chunks of river bank, plants and all, avalanche into the river.

Creepy snake or not, exhaustion caught up with me and I slipped in and out of a restless sleep filled with nightmarish images. The only hope came from a pair of playful river dolphins tracking our progress. They seemed to smile encouragement at me and I liked them all the more when the snake shrunk from them. Still, I can't be sure if I didn't dream that part too.

I lost all track of time and couldn't say for sure, but figured we had floated down the river for most of the night before the boat was beached just before dawn.

In the predawn light I saw a group of heron fishing near the bank. Their food supply was so plentiful they would grab a fish in their beaks and then inspect the variety of their catch before making a snap decision whether they wanted to eat it or throw it back.

There was something else moving in the water

among the heron that I couldn't quite make out at first. It wasn't until one of the crocodiles lifted its snout wide and then abruptly snapped it shut on an unsuspecting fish that I figured it out. I couldn't help but wonder why the crocodiles left the heron alone. Fishing side by side, the two creatures made for very strange companions.

We made a wide berth around the crocodiles on our way to the shore. Once we were on the bank, Voodoo Girl led us into the jungle. There was no apparent trail. Still, we moved at a blistering pace through the dense foliage. She seemed to follow an unseen path of least resistance. We continued to travel at a brutal pace. Foot sore and weary, I focused on my breath.

Ch'ing's voice echoed from the past telling me, "Just breathe. Take one breath at a time. Nothing else matters."

It helped. I felt a sense of well-being spread to the deepest parts of my inner self. Despite the desperate circumstance, I began to feel calm within minutes of the hike. The trail does that to me. An old forest is a peaceful place. It tends to its own needs, free of human manipulation. It's like a cathedral where the hand of God is within reach.

Finally, Voodoo Girl stopped next to a mountain stream. She scanned the surrounding jungle. Satisfied, she dropped to her knees and slowly bent toward the water. I expected her to scoop it with her hands, but she began lapping it up like a cat. No one else moved toward the stream until she had her fill.

Then one at a time, they drank. I was the last. When my turn finally came, I gratefully dropped to my knees and scooped a handful of cool water. In the moonlight I could see the stream was clear, like glass.

I heard the flutter of wings. A bat swooped in, nabbed a small fish, and abruptly changed course to avoid a head on collision with me. I know bats aren't the evil creatures portrayed in Dracula movies, but it's hard not to get little freaked out when I see one swoop in at eye level.

When I finished, I turned toward the others and was greeted by the anaconda's cold eyes. I recoiled and shifted my gaze to Voodoo Girl. She looked at me like food. No relief there.

After we drank from the stream, I thought we would rest for a while, but Voodoo Girl resumed her brutal pace into the depths of the jungle. There was a sense of urgency, as if she was in a hurry to get to a safe place.

She never stopped scanning our surroundings and sniffing the air. I wondered what she feared might be lurking in the jungle. Although I saw no outward signs of danger, I could feel unseen eyes watching. Someone or something was following us.

We were deep into the wilderness when the temperature began to drop. I heard a deep rumble that sounded like a lion from an old Tarzan movie. Of course there are no lions in the Amazon rainforest, but there are Jaguars. Then I saw the unmistakable flash of lightening and it began to rain.

Suddenly, the anaconda whipped its head to the side. Voodoo Girl froze. Swat Cop rapidly scanned the surrounding bush. There was a wild animal look in his eyes. Wife Beater dropped into a crouch. The anaconda slithered off her shoulders and disappeared into the forest.

Swat Cop raised his gun in my direction and shouted, "Die gringo devil."

Having guns pointed in my face was becoming annoyingly familiar. I heard the twang almost the same instant that an arrow pierced his throat and silenced him. Swat Cop crumbled to his knees without firing a shot.

Voodoo Girl hissed. For the first time I saw her teeth. My God, it looked like a cat's mouth. She sprung toward the cover of the jungle but a dart in the neck stopped her cold.

Wife Beater was flat on the ground. Damned if she wasn't slithering like a snake, moving in the same direction as the anaconda. A spear between the shoulder blades pinned her to the ground where she lay in pool of dark blood.

They were all dead. Only I remained standing. The forest began to close in on me. There was a flash of lightening. Faces slowly emerged from the shifting shadows.

Painted warriors carrying Stone Age weapons surrounded me. Other than a few feathers and beads, they were naked. They were also huge. I estimated they were nearly seven feet tall and packed with muscle.

Naked or not, these Amazons looked deadly, even the women…correction, especially the women. When you meet a tiger in the jungle, you don't check its private parts to see whether it is male or female. It's a tiger and you better respect it because all tigers, regardless of gender, are dangerous.

These naked giants had just killed three people. Would they kill me too? No one spoke. We waited.

Finally, an ageless man broke the circle of warriors and moved toward me. I say ageless, not because he was elderly. In fact he looked to be in his mid-twenties. My assessment had more to do with the way he carried himself. It spoke volumes. This man was wise. It was the kind of wisdom that comes from years of experience and it made him seem ancient. Like he was an old soul.

He was shorter than the others, maybe six and a half feet tall, give or take an inch or two. The spear in his left hand was at least a foot taller. He may have been shorter than the others, but he had a bigger presence.

Coal black hair flowed down his back and reached just below his shoulder blades. His head was perfectly symmetrical, like the letter "O" and crowned with yellow and green feathers. The only other thing he wore were strips of white fabric wrapped around his lower legs and blue fabric around his biceps. His brown skin was painted red on the right side of his body and black on the left.

The warrior stopped inches from me and peered into my eyes. I figured he invaded my personal space for a good reason, so I returned his gaze in search of my own answers. What I found were surprisingly kind eyes. This man was a gentle soul.

Whatever he was looking for, he found. In one swift movement, he unsheathed his knife and cut the rope from my hands. As I rubbed circulation back into my wrists, the warrior gracefully swept his arm toward the others and spoke for the first time in perfect English.

"We are the Guardians," he said.

They bowed their heads in unison.

He placed his hand over his heart and said, "I am called Teekal."

"My name is Grant," I said.

Teekal placed his hand over my heart and said, "Welcome to the gateway, Grant."

One by one, the rest of the group stepped forward and introduced themselves in a similar manner. I'm normally good with names, but theirs were so unusual I quickly gave up trying to remember them. When the introductions were completed, Teekal motioned me to follow him deeper into the jungle.

I pointed in the opposite direction.

"Thank you for your help, but I have to get back to Manaus," I said. "Can someone show me the way back to the river?"

"What you seek is in this direction," said Teekal.

Without another word he led the group of warriors into the jungle. I briefly considered blazing my own trail in the opposite direction, but I was far from home and hopelessly lost. There was also a part of me that knew I could trust them, so without further hesitation, I followed the Guardians to an uncertain outcome.

The rain was falling steadily, but I was accustomed to hiking in the rain. Still, it wasn't easy to keep up with them. The Guardians moved at a blistering pace in the dark jungle and somehow blended in as if they were protected by a space age cloaking device.

At first I wanted to slow down and carefully pick my way through the darkness, but I knew they would have gone off and left me there if I had. Instead, I had to use my intuition like it had never been used before, trusting that each blind step was exactly where it needed to be.

Focused on each step, I was completely immersed in the here and now. Time disappeared. For the duration of the hike, there was nowhere else but here.

As my awareness heightened, I sensed something was shadowing our movements. I couldn't see or hear it, but I felt it all the same. The warriors showed no signs of concern. These people belonged to the jungle.

When I thought I couldn't take another step, we finally stopped. One of the women took my hand and led me to an open-air dwelling that I hadn't even realized we'd come to. It blended well with the forest and was nearly invisible. Inside I heard the sounds of sleep. She pointed in the direction of an empty hammock. I gratefully collapsed into it and fell immediately into a deep sleep.

CHAPTER 6

I awoke to the touch of a warm body cuddled next to me. It was still night, but the jungle was glowing softly with moonlight. Some of the light managed to penetrate the shelter, revealing the faint outlines of six other hammocks stuffed with sleeping bodies.

I didn't know this place and tried to remember how I got here. The initial confusion passed and yesterday's events flooded my mind. Not sure what to make of it, I thought of getting up and sorting it all out, but the need for sleep won out and I closed my eyes once again.

Without clocks, I had no way of knowing how long I slept before a nagging bladder interrupted a sexy dream where I saw Ginny standing at the edge of my bed. Her eyes were soft and luminous. Neither of us spoke. She reached behind and slowly unzipped her black cocktail dress. As it began to slide down her shoulder, I awoke from the dream with a full bladder screaming for release.

I didn't want to get up. Instead I lay there thinking about Ginny. She was in trouble. I could feel it. I needed to help her…to rescue her, but had no way of knowing how to find her in the vast Rainforest.

My bladder refused to be ignored. I started to groan, but stopped. No sense in waking the others. Instead, I slowly opened my eyes. A beam of moonlight cut across the shelter. I was alone in the hammock. Whoever was sleeping next to me earlier had left.

As I reluctantly swung my feet to the ground, it occurred to me that I was in a primitive place without the luxury of a bathroom down the hall. I would have to make my way by moonlight to the edge of the jungle before I could relieve the pressure on my bladder.

With a sigh, I tiptoed into the night. When I reached the tree line, I counted another twenty paces before stopping next to a chest high bush with leaves as big as watermelons to pee. Not that anyone else was awake, but I figured the broad leaves would insure privacy while I tended to business.

I'm an experienced backpacker and have spent many nights in the backcountry. Unlike some of my city dwelling friends, I find the forest's night sounds soothing. The symphony of sound I heard as I tended to nature was unique to the Amazon Rainforest.

For the first time since I arrived, I could relax

and let the forest's music carry me where it would, but it was short lived. The music abruptly stopped. The jungle became deathly still. As I stood there shaking the last few drops, I was suddenly knocked to the ground. Somebody had ambushed me.

A hundred razor sharp teeth glinted in the moonlight. The attacker hissed. Holy cow, not somebody, but something and it was huge. All I could see was a field of white and too many teeth to count.

The strike came fast. I was groggy from the blow and flat on my back. A heavy weight pressed me into the earth. Not much time or room for a maneuver. Instinctively, I shifted my head at the last second. Teeth sank into my left shoulder.

I tried to lift my right arm, but something heavy pinned it against my chest. That's not good. My left hand flew to the source of pain. I punched it. The teeth sunk deeper. It hurt like hell. I tried to pry it off, but it was bigger than my hand. We started rolling. I couldn't quite get a grip on it.

I felt a sharp pain in my ribs. Damn, it was squeezing the breath out of me. I pushed back. It squeezed tighter. I was strong. It was stronger. Where did all the oxygen go? It was hard to breathe. I tried to shout, but nothing came out except a muffled moan.

I panicked. In my fumbling to get a hold of it, I felt something soft. It was the corner of an eye. The squeezing intensified. Desperate, I shoved a finger in as far as I could. The eye popped out. The bite released and the ambusher tried to pull away, but I pressed its head firmly against my shoulder.

I was pissed now and shouted, "Die…die…die a painful death…die…die..."

It rolled us across the jungle floor. Something sharp, maybe a rock, jabbed into my hip. Still, I held firm and began rotating my finger inside of its head. I felt a shock. It ran from my finger and pulsated throughout my body. When it hit my head I saw white light and then everything went dark.

I tried to claw myself out of the darkness, but the weight of it was too much. Finally, I accepted the inevitable and relaxed. So this is how it ends, a grave less death in the middle of the jungle, far from home, without friends or family to see me off.

I was surrounded by darkness and expected to see a light that I could move toward, but it never appeared. There was only darkness and it seemed to extend forever into eternity.

I don't know how much time passed before I heard a voice. It was a welcome break from the nothingness. The crushing weight was gone and I could breathe again. The voice came louder. It was a woman I heard and she was speaking soothingly, like you would to a wounded animal.

"Open your eyes," she said.

It seemed like a good idea and I wanted to open them, but there was a disconnect between desire and action.

"Aaawk, open your eyes peckerwood," squawked Bird.

I thought it was weird how I kept hearing my dad's macaw way out here in the middle of nowhere. I chalked it up to snake venom and tried to go back to sleep.

A man whispered, "The serpent is dead."

Another voice, "It is him."

When I realized these people weren't going to let me rest, I opened my eyes and focused on the face leaning over me. It was soft and feminine, framed by long black hair. I could see compassion in her luminous brown eyes. There was something else in them too…ancient wisdom, I thought weirdly.

I'm pretty sure she had been the one in my bed earlier. She was tall like the others and packed with muscle. Her hips and breasts were round and proportionate to each other in a classic hourglass way. She was nude and in the light of the full moon, I could see that her brown skin was flawless.

There was a self-possessed air about her that seemed regal to me. At first I assumed she was a leader, but when I shifted my gaze to the small crowd that formed behind her, I could see they were not followers. None of them showed any sign they were the subjects of a master.

"How extraordinary," I whispered. "Each and every one of you is clearly in charge of yourself."

"As it should be," she said. "Do you remember me?"

I nodded.

"You were in the hammock with me earlier," I answered.

She smiled. "Yes, but we met earlier," she said.

It took a moment, but I remembered seeing her with the warriors who rescued me from the freaks. The face paint had been washed away, but it was her. I nodded.

"I'm sorry I don't remember your name," I said.

"My name is Layah," she said. "Let us help you with your injuries."

Gentle hands cleaned my wounds. I intended to nod in assent, but felt a sharp pain and grimaced instead.

A man handed me a cup saying, "Drink."

When I raised an eyebrow, he grinned and

said, "Great Mother."

I had no idea what he meant. I sniffed and found it to be pleasantly aromatic. It smelled faintly of the jungle around us and what I imagine sunshine would smell like if it had a smell.

He put his hand to his mouth and tilted his head back. I took a sip. It was neither hot nor cold and tasted odd. It wasn't odd in a bad way...but rather odd because it was beyond my experience. It seemed to be sweet, sour, salty, and bitter all at the same time.

My body's reaction to the sip was surprising. I instantly craved the rest of the liquid and drank it down without hesitation.

"Rest now," said Layah.

The remainder of the night was uneventful. The next morning I felt rested, but extremely weird. I tingled, as if unimpeded electrical current flowed through me. It wasn't unpleasant...just unusual.

I remembered the snake bite and checked my shoulder. There was no sign of injury. How could that be? The damn anaconda ripped out a huge hunk of flesh.

I also cracked another rib in last night's battle with the snake. That made two cracked ribs over the last few days, the other coming from a hard kick delivered by Slotter, the psycho ex-Special

Forces chick, disguised as a Tibetan monk. I gently pressed against both ribs. There was no pain…nothing.

I checked my gunshot wounds. The first was nothing more than a scratch that I received while guarding Padma. He is one of those unassuming people you'd never think could become a celebrity, but when he wrote a book about paradise the world fell in love with his ideas about peace and happiness.

At the time, I wasn't sure why anybody thought he needed a bodyguard. As it turned out, things got crazy when he tried to reveal the secret of long life to an auditorium full of fans hungry for something meaningful. Instead of Padma's description of a land of peace and plenty, gunshot blasts filled the auditorium.

A lot of people died, but not from bullet wounds. The official reason given for their deaths was an accidental gas leak, but it sure looked like they were locked inside to me. I don't think it was an accident.

The second gunshot wound was far more serious. I took a bullet in the back trying to rescue Ginny from Slotter, the Special Forces chick who broke my rib.

Despite all of that, I felt great. I was the walking wounded when I arrived in Brazil. Now there wasn't a sore bone in my body. The

Guardians gave me medicine that worked wonders on my injuries and I needed to know what else it could heal.

Was this the medicine Pony Tail had given to Ginny and Uncle Jim? If so, could it be used to help my mother? She has been a prisoner of her bed for twenty years, a paraplegic, robbed of the life she was meant to have by a hit-and-run driver. No matter how slim the chance, I needed to explore the possibility this medicine could heal her.

For now though, my rumbling stomach reminded me it had been more than twenty-four hours since I last had something to eat. I tried to swallow, but my throat was parched. I didn't know if it was meal time for the Guardians, but I needed food and water.

I looked around for signs of food, but the shelter was empty except for a beam of sunlight splitting the space. A cool breeze drifted across my skin. Other than goose bumps, I was naked. I arrived fully clothed and had no memory of undressing.

I scanned the room for my clothes. They were nowhere in sight. The only thing I could use to cover myself was a basket. The thought of hiding behind a basket seemed silly around a bunch of naked people, so I abandoned the idea.

As I was about to step into the light, I

suddenly stopped. My entire body was shaking. I couldn't remember being this scared, except maybe when I was a kid and the Fat Lady caught me playing a game of show me yours with her daughter, Ginny. Some wounds seem to resist healing.

Public nudity is definitely not my thing. It took every ounce of courage I had to leave the shelter, but I did it. Squaring my shoulders, I abandoned the shadows and stepped into the morning light.

I stood in a small clearing surrounded by a group of open aired lodges. The roofs were constructed from palms and connected together to form a ring around a central fire pit. The location of the four cardinal points were marked on the edge of the pit. The overall effect was a circle within a circle.

Looking out from the center of the circle was a twenty foot clear space buffering the lodges from the surrounding jungle. I imagine it also provided light and security for the Guardians.

The small village reminded me of a scene from an old movie and I half expected to see a feral man-ape swinging from limb to limb in the treetops. I could almost hear his voice calling to the jungle, "aweuaauaawe."

I was starting to feel comfortable, when I saw a one-eyed snake. My blood ran cold. It was huge…the biggest damn snake I've ever seen…at least a hundred feet long.

"Aaawk, don't be afraid," squawked Bird. "It's as dead as a doornail."

"I had no idea they got that big," I muttered.

"There are giants among us," said a woman's voice.

"Must be something in the water," I said.

"Aaawk, we grow 'em big around here, for sure," said Bird.

"Yes," said the woman.

"The damn thing almost killed me," I said.

"This was once a great serpent," she said. "Now she belongs to you."

I tore my eyes from the beast. Standing close enough that our hips almost touched was Layah. On her shoulder, sat Dad's macaw. As long as I can remember the only name he ever had was Bird. Except lately, he had taken to calling himself, Ponce.

"I don't understand," I said.

"You survived a battle with a powerful enemy," she said. "The serpent's spirit is now a part of you."

"A part of me?" I murmured.

She nodded.

"Aaawk, are you going to say hello or just keep pretending I'm not here," squawked Bird.

Bird was a hemisphere away in Louisville.

Since he had to be some kind of hallucination, I ignored him. On the other hand, the snake was as real as it gets.

I've always hated snakes. I'm not exactly sure why, but I was raised on the biblical story of Eve's temptation and her fall from grace. Thanks to the serpent's lies, paradise was lost and mankind was left to toil and suffer. It was unthinkable that I was the serpent.

"What if I don't want a snake's spirit inside of me?" I asked.

"Where is the me that is separate from the serpent?" asked Layah.

"You sound like a friend of mine," I said with a laugh.

"Your friend must be very wise," giggled Layah.

"Aaawk, I'm the smartest bird that ever was or ever will be, Toots," said Bird.

Layah stroked the side of Bird's ample beak and said in soothing tone of voice, "Why you're not a bird at all, Ponce."

"If Bird isn't really a bird, then what is he?" I asked.

Bird leaned slowly in my direction as if he intended to reveal a great secret and then suddenly bit the tip of my nose. It hurt like hell and I'm pretty sure he drew blood.

"Aaawk, if you want to see my true nature,

peckerwood, then open your eyes," said Bird. "Or at least pay attention to the clues."

I covered my nose to protect it from a second assault and said, "Stop that, Bird."

"No need to get violent, Ponce," said Layah. "I think Grant was talking about someone else."

I checked my nose for signs of blood and was relieved to find it clean.

"I was talking about Ch'ing," I grumbled.

"Aaawk, Ch'ing, Ch'ing, always Ch'ing," said Bird. "It's about time this peckerwood gave me a little respect too."

I swatted at Bird, but he managed to duck at the last minute. I could be mistaken, but I think he hissed at me. Then again, it could be I only imagined I heard a hiss when I got an unobstructed look at the one eyed snakeskin when he ducked.

"The serpent is a deceiver," I said. "That's not something I want inside of me."

"Are you open-minded?" asked Layah.

"I like to believe so," I answered.

"Aaawk, open-minded my ass," said Bird. I bet your wife would have a different opinion on that subject."

Layah raised an eyebrow, but didn't ask Bird what he meant.

Instead she said to me, "If you're open-minded, then guard against assumptions about the serpent. Kundalini is the path to freedom."

"What do you mean?" I asked.

"There is latent energy stored at the base of the spine, like a sleeping serpent coiled around the sacrum," answered Layah. "It is called, Kundalini. When it awakens, it spirals up the spine, energizing each aspect of your life. In the process, you become the person you were destined to be."

Bird ripped a noisy fart and screeched, "Aaawk, I got your sacral energy right here. Take a deep breath and feel the power of this bird."

"Really Bird?" I said.

Surprisingly, Bird looked a little embarrassed by his own behavior. That had to be a first. As I turned my attention back to Layah, I couldn't help but wonder if it wasn't the end-times.

"Aaawk, that's exactly what it is," said Bird.

I wasn't sure if he was still talking about the power of his fart or the end-times. I decided to ignore him. I mean…really…as if he could actually read my mind.

"Kundalini sounds something like the energy work I practice," I said to Layah. "We call it Chi Kung."

"Don't get caught up in terminology," said Layah. "It makes no difference what we call it, the life force is the same."

"It's not just terminology," I said. "We collect

and store energy in our lower abdomen, a place we call the Tan Tien. It sounds to me like your practice draws energy from that area."

"Truth lies in the common ground, but it can also be found in our differences," said Layah.

"It seems to me that the two practices are very different," I said. "Maybe I could see the common ground better if I knew a little more about your practice. You said something about awakening Kundalini. How is that accomplished?"

Layah flashed a radiant smile and said, "Ahhh…you're listening. Good. You begin at the beginning, of course. The first aim of meditation is to quiet the mind's incessant chatter. This is best accomplished by opening the mind until it quiets of its own accord. I like to think of it like opening a window and letting a cool breeze clear the air inside of the room."

I looked around and noted that none of the buildings in this tiny village had windows. In fact they had no doors or walls for that matter. They were completely open.

"You do air it out," I said cutting my eyes to Bird.

"The best practice is to remember what is good for the inside is also good on the outside," said Layah. "It reconciles the incongruent aspects of life."

"What do you mean?" I asked.

People are often divided against themselves," said Layah. "They say they want one thing, but do the opposite. When the mind is faced with an incongruity, such as a paradoxical problem, it's best to reconcile that or else the mind will grab hold of the first thing that makes any sense."

Bird fluttered off with a squawk.

I was not only having trouble with the idea that part of me was a snake, it was pretty damn weird having a spiritual discussion in the nude. On top of that, the snake skin drying in the sun added to the bizarre scene. It seemed primitive to me...almost barbaric and not spiritual at all.

I was uncomfortable being around someone stripped of outer clothing. Likewise, the snake was stripped of everything on the inside that makes up a living creature. How that had anything to do with me was unclear...and trying to sort it out gave me the first hint of a headache.

"What purpose does saving the skin serve?" I asked.

"This one is special," said Layah.

"How is it special?" I asked.

She seemed to search my face for something before answering.

"This creature is more than a dangerous beast," she said. "You might say it is supernatural."

I took another look at the huge snake and to my chagrin began shaking. It embarrassed me. I tried to control it and failed.

"It must be a chill," I said.

Layah wrapped me in a warm hug.

"You are very brave," she said softly.

At six feet, I was at least a head shorter then her. Still, my face shouldn't have ended up between her breasts like it did. I told myself she coaxed it there in a motherly way, but my reaction was not familial.

My response to her touch mortified me. What is even worse, it attracted the attention of a group of women. I hadn't thought they were paying any attention to us, since they were circling the fire, hand in hand, while chanting in a strange tongue. It embarrassed me when they stopped and openly stared. The tallest one whispered something to the others and they all began giggling like school girls.

A man I recognized from the night before smiled and waved me over. He was roughly the same height as Layah, maybe a tad shorter at 6'7". Like her, his skin was smooth and unblemished. His smiling face was wrinkle free, but his eyes also seemed ancient. By ancient I don't mean tired. Instead, they were infinitely wise. We've all heard the term "Old Soul" before, but he really fit the bill.

Layah gave me a little push in his direction. Smiling, I walked over to join him near the fire.

"That's a little embarrassing," I said.

It hardly seemed possible, but his smile widened a bit more.

In a voice we usually reserve for small children, he asked, "What do you find embarrassing?"

I opened my mouth to answer, but nothing came out. How do you explain "embarrassment" to someone who is so obviously comfortable in their own skin? It was as if we spoke a different emotional language. I wasn't certain yet, but I think I liked his language better.

I shrugged and said, "I'm Grant. I think we met last night. Isn't your name Teekal."

A wide grin filled his face.

"Yes, I'm Teekal," he said. "You must be hungry."

He offered me a wooden bowl filled with creamy porridge. Unfamiliar fruit, nuts, and seeds were stirred in. I expected it to be bland, but it was delicious. In fact, it was the best thing I've ever eaten. A mug of rich dark roasted cowboy coffee and cocoa followed. Yummmm!

"Good," he said.

I nodded. He waited as I ate and drank the food he provided. Even though we didn't speak during the meal, it didn't feel awkward and I wasn't hurried.

After I swallowed the last bite, he asked if I wanted more. Good food has a way of arousing greed, but not this meal. I was satisfied on many levels and declined his offer. What I wanted instead, were answers.

"Why do you call yourself the Guardians?" I asked.

"It's who we are," he answered. "We guard the gateway."

"The gateway to what?" I asked.

"Paradise," he answered.

I looked around. This remote part of the Amazon Rainforest was beautiful and you could call it "Paradise," but I sensed he was talking about something else, something more mysterious and hidden from view. I wanted to ask more about it, but my gut told me a direct approach would only push it further out of view. It was time for a new line of questions.

"Do you know what happened to my clothes?" I asked.

He scrunched up his nose in distaste and said, "Smell bad."

Nodding toward the fire he added, "I burned them."

"Damn," I murmured.

"Come, you smell bad too and we have just what is needed to fix it," he said.

He turned and walked toward a path leading into the jungle. I stuck my nose in my armpit and breathed deeply. He was right. I smelled ripe and hoped he didn't plan to burn me too.

I had a vision of myself being slow cooked over an open fire. I didn't think I would be very appetizing and I had to laugh out loud. He looked over his shoulder at me and grinned. I trusted him.

He led us down to a stream and we waded into the center. It was an easy walk since the stream flowed across a sheet of bedrock that curved up the north bank like a breaking wave forming a rock shelter. The opposite bank was lined with a wide variety of flowers, some as big as your head, mixed with ferns, palms, and broad leaf plants.

I wasn't familiar with the vegetation, but overall it reminded me of the bank of the many streams and rivers I had paddled over the years. The only exception was the wide variety of tropical flowers that were home to an astonishing number of butterflies. The most interesting flower looked like a set of large red painted hooker lips. I had never seen anything like it.

The water was never much deeper than just below my knees. Still, I continuously scanned it for fish. I wasn't interested in catching them for food; instead I couldn't get images of man eating piranha out of my mind. Each time I saw a fish,

I tensed up thinking it might try to take a bite out of me.

After I saw a snake, I immediately stopped worrying about the fish and my ample imagination ran wild with the dangers of snake bites. It was fueled by a guy I met on a backpacking trip a few years earlier who told me he had spent years in the back country only to be bitten by a snake in his own back yard. With a disgusted expression he told me the anti-venom cost him $28,000.00 dollars a dose.

I didn't want to believe the medicine actually cost that much, but given the way the healthcare industry has run amuck, I'm sure he was telling the truth. In any event, I sure didn't want to test it. Of course, I knew the chance of getting to a hospital in time from this remote location was virtually nil. I was really getting tired of snakes.

In the corner of my eye I saw a flash of movement and turned just in time to see a dragon faced toad, nearly as big as a dinner plate, leap from the bank and splash into a pool next to a fallen log.

Even though I was experienced in the backcountry, I don't remember ever being so skittish about the wildlife. It was time to take it down a notch, so I took a deep breath and focused on the beauty that surrounded me. It helped. Once I started paying attention to how good the cool water felt, I began to calm down. I liked this place.

After a short walk, we came to a confluence of two streams. Teekal headed up the second stream which led into a bowl shaped area formed by rock shelters on three sides. A twenty foot water fall emptied into a swimming hole filled with frolicking swimmers.

The fourth side of the bowl was dominated by a beach filled with coral colored sand where sunbathers were stretched out napping or engaged in various forms of play.

There was steam rising on the backside of the beach that I initially mistook as smoke. Upon closer examination, I saw about twenty people soaking in a hot spring. The bathers smiled and waved me in. What the hell, I thought. I figured a bath would feel great. So, I waded into the hot water.

At its deepest point, it rose to my chest. It was there that I came to a rest. It felt wonderful. The water was fragrant, a little like rosemary and a second scent I couldn't quite pinpoint, but was hauntingly familiar. It was calming to the mind and soothing to the skin. No wonder everyone in the hot springs looked so mellow.

The waterfall crowd was more playful. They laughed and frolicked with each other. There was no indication they felt self-conscious about their nudity. In fact, no one seemed to give it a second thought. I didn't see any aggressive behavior in their play. They seemed so different than the warriors who had killed so efficiently the night before. I never heard a cross word spoken. Their laughter penetrated deeply. It was music to my soul.

Folks moved back and forth from the hot springs to the waterfall, alternating hot and cold. Feeling hot, I decided to switch pools. The waterfall was cold and refreshing. I began to laugh, slowly at first, and then uncontrollably. It felt so good to be alive.

I spent the next few hours going back and forth between the two pools. I smiled and chatted with them from time to time, but mostly I communed with my inner self.

The sun had reached its apex and begun its descent toward the western horizon when I noticed everyone had left. I was beginning to feel whole again. Like Congressional pork that piggy backs onto a new bill, the urgency to find Ginny attached itself to my sense of well-being.

I resolved to ask to be guided out of the jungle first thing in the morning.

CHAPTER 7

Ham sized chunks of flesh sizzled over an open pit at the center of the village. The meat looked unfamiliar, but smelled delicious. For some reason, I had pegged these people as vegetarians and wondered what manner of beast they were barbequing. When my eyes fell on the snake skin curing in the sun, I began to suspect we were having slow roasted Anaconda for dinner. Ughhh...

The villagers wandered in with decorative baskets filled with fruit, vegetables, and flat bread. The food was set on low tables arranged around the central fire pit. Garlands of pink and white flowers softened the setting and gave the evening meal a festive feel.

There were a few odd pets, but I hesitate to call them that. No one acted as if they owned them. It seemed more like they just wanted to hang out with the Guardians and each other. For example, a playful monkey with orange hair and black eyes trimmed in white rode around the camp on the back of Jaguar. The big cat didn't seem to mind when the monkey tugged on his whiskers and ears. In fact, I'm pretty sure I heard him purring.

There were many other creatures that were so colorful and exotic the place felt a little like nature's art gallery. One of my favorites was a little guy that looked like a mix between a caterpillar and bright blue cotton candy.

He had a voracious appetite and could easily consume several times his weight in a short time. Not surprisingly, his favorite food was a blue leaf vine that climbed many of the trees near the Guardian's swimming hole.

I was deep in the Amazon Rainforest and didn't have a clue how to find my way home. It felt wonderful to be lost in this wild place. It occurred to me that these primitive people were far more civilized than anyone at home. In fact, I felt more at home here than I did at home.

People watching is one of my favorite pastimes. This was the first time the entire community was gathered together in my presence. They were as interesting as any group of people I have ever encountered, but something bothered me about them that I couldn't quite put a finger on at first. Then it hit me. There was no diversity in this crowd.

While I wouldn't go so far as to say they all looked alike, what was clearly evident was they were all young and beautiful. Not one of them showed any sign of being older than twenty-five. In fact, the more I thought about it, they all appeared to be in their mid-twenties.

There were no children, teenagers, middle aged adults, or seniors. How could that be, I wondered. Absent foul play, it seemed impossible.

Likewise, none of them were overweight, handicapped, or had any visible scars. They were all brown skinned, healthy and gorgeous. Each and every one of them was physically fit and attractive. Not a single exception. I had never seen anything like it and couldn't make any sense of it.

Finally, and maybe more importantly, they all seemed cheerful and well-adjusted. If I hadn't seen them wipe out my creepy captors in a blink of an eye, I would say they didn't have a violent bone in any of their beautiful bodies.

There was a loving gentleness between them that I had rarely seen between two people, let alone an entire group of thirty or more. It was a beautiful thing to witness and as I watched it, something deep inside of me shifted. I could feel it and it felt right, as if I had been out of focus and suddenly I could see everything more clearly.

That's when I felt something else that was even more remarkable. It was like I had a big goofy grin that was as much on the inside as the outside. This inner smile can best be described as contentment. I felt as if everything was as it should be. The world was the way it needed to be and I was right with it…perfect just as I am.

A smiling woman approached and handed me a stone carved mug of herbal tea.

"You have a beautiful smile," she said. "It radiates from your true nature."

"Thank you," I said. "This place brings out the best in me. I like it here."

After we introduced ourselves, I pointed toward the meat sizzling over the fire pit and raised an eyebrow.

"We rarely eat meat and when we do, it's in small quantities, but this is a special occasion," she said.

"What's the occasion?" I asked.

"We are celebrating the end of an era," she answered.

I raised my mug and offered a simple toast.

"To new beginnings," I said.

After she excused herself, I stood alone in a beam of the waning sunlight and enjoyed the bliss rippling through me like gentle waves kissing the shore. The moment of peace was interrupted by a big commotion at the edge of the village. It wasn't a negative buzz. Instead, everyone seemed excited and happy.

I looked in the direction of the commotion,

but my view was partially blocked by the Guardians. I couldn't quite make out what was going on. A woman obstructing the view moved slightly and I caught a glimpse of a man walking into the village.

Except for the lack of a battle axe, the newcomer looked like central casting's version of a Viking warrior. This man had fought and won a few battles in his lifetime. It showed in the way he carried himself.

In addition to the fighter's body language, there was deep intelligence in his eyes. This guy was formidable. He was smart, tall, muscular, and did I mention, very blond. I guessed him to be about my age, maybe twenty-eight or so.

Unlike the Guardians, Mr. Viking was fully clothed. In this place it seemed wrong somehow. He was wearing something that looked like homemade chaps and a vest. The bottoms of his feet were protected with sandals fashioned from some sort of roughhewn rope similar to the rope that my captors had used to bind my wrists.

Layah bounded in his direction and took a flying leap into his arms. Given she was nearly seven feet tall and packed with muscle, it was no small feat that he actually caught this Amazon Woman in mid-air and pressed her high over his head.

The other Guardians showered him with

greetings, hugs, and kisses. Once the love fest was over, his expression shifted to something far more serious. The Guardians grew silent as he spoke in a language I didn't understand.

When Mr. Viking finished speaking, everyone scattered. There was a bustle of activity as they returned one by one with faces painted for war and weapons in hand. Without a word, they moved quietly into the forest.

I didn't have a clue what had just happened and didn't know whether I should stay put or follow them. I needed to find Ginny. My gut told me time was running out for her. It was also clear that I couldn't do it alone, so I followed them.

We ran silently through the thick foliage for nearly an hour without a break. The big Viking must have been near the front of the group because I hadn't seen him since we started. There were a few questions I wanted to ask, but couldn't figure out a diplomatic way to do it. Besides, the pace was blistering and I was focused on keeping up with everyone else.

Finally, we took a break and I found a spot to rest on a bed of hooker's green moss within arm's reach of a bubbling brook. I leaned back and rested my eyes. I must have dozed because someone woke me with a shake. Startled, I opened my eyes to see Layah offering me food and water.

"You must keep up your strength," she said.

I took her offering and munched quietly on something that tasted like a cross between a fruit cake and a granola bar, only better. The big Viking walked by and I figured it was a good time to ask a few questions.

I pointed toward Mr. Viking and asked, "Who is he?"

"I think you would call him my husband," she answered.

That surprised me, because none of these people behaved like the married people I knew. Instead, they treated everyone in the group with a level of love and respect, the likes of which I had never seen before.

I wanted to ask more about the Viking, but for now, that would have to wait. I had other, more pressing questions I wanted to ask.

"Where are we going?" I asked.

Before Layah could answer my question, the group stood on some unspoken command. Layah gave me a little shake of the head and rose with them. Without another word, we continued the journey. My questions would have to wait.

I didn't have a clue how I was going to find Ginny in this vast place. My only lead was in Manaus. I needed to return to her factory and speak with her security chief, Victor Branco, since he was somehow connected to the events at the Center.

We ran in silence for another hour before coming to a halt. There was a brief discussion between Layah and the Big Viking. Layah nodded before trotting off ahead. I slid over to Teekal and asked him where she was going.

"To find a weakness," he whispered.

I wanted to ask more questions, but he put a finger to his lips and shook his head. There was nothing to do, but wait. Which is exactly what we did for about thirty minutes, when Layah returned.

There was another whispered discussion, before the group began to move quietly in the direction Layah had traveled. Teekal motioned for me to remain, but that only lasted for a couple of minutes before I began to feel restless and decided to follow anyway.

I figured it would be easy to catch up with them, but the warriors had vanished. Initially, I followed their example and moved as quietly as I could through the jungle, but once I realized they were nowhere in sight, the likelihood I'd get lost filled me with panic. The Amazon Rainforest is huge, over two million square miles, and I was a stranger here.

By the time I stumbled through the undergrowth and into a small clearing, I was nearly as loud as a freight train. I knew I had made a huge mistake in not listening to Teekal when I found myself looking down the barrel of a gun.

CHAPTER 8

Lately everyone wanted to point a damn gun at me, and sadly, I was getting used to it. The handgun was held thug style, as if it was her habit to intimidate as much as kill. Hard eyes delivered a chilling message that didn't need to be spoken. It seemed unlikely she could say it anyway, since her jaw was clamped tight around a pitiless mouth. There wasn't a bit of softness in her face that I could see.

She wore camo pants, combat boots, and a purple sequined tube top. A tie-dyed bandana with the peace sign in the center of her forehead completed her cartoonish appearance.

There was something that wasn't quite right about Camo Girl that I couldn't quite put a finger on. She appeared to be hard to the core, but it didn't fit. My years of martial arts training told me she was no fighter. In another world she could have been a Victoria Secrets model. If it wasn't for the 9mm and hard expression, it would have been hard to take her seriously.

Still, there was no doubt in my mind that she had lived a hard and violent life. The disturbing thing was I knew that unless something happened real fast, I was destined for a violent ending.

I raised hands in the universal sign of surrender and said, "Easy, I'm just looking for my friends."

Camo Girl said nothing. It never occurred to me until that moment that she didn't speak English. In fact, for the first time I began to wonder how the Guardians, who lived in an isolated village deep in the Amazon jungle, spoke English like it was their own.

Her coal black hair was pulled back tight, heightening her high cheekbones and almond shaped eyes. She wore it as a long braid pulled over her shoulder where it was left to fall in a curve around her ample breast.

I did a double take when it moved. About the time I was sure it was only my imagination, it twitched like a cat's tail. You know your life has taken a strange turn when you begin to assume that just because something is odd, it has a supernatural explanation, like maybe Camo Girl was part jungle cat.

"Would you please stop that?" she said.

As I wondered what the hell she was talking about, a face popped over her shoulder. I sure as hell didn't expect to see my best friend Eric, but that's who appeared from the bushes. Being

Eric, he couldn't resist tugging on her pig tail like a school boy.

"I was just messing with Grant," he said.

"You know this guy?" she asked.

"Yeah, you can put the gun down," he said. "This is the rascal I've been looking for."

"What took you so long?" I asked.

"Ingrate," he said. "The party woke me from my siesta," said Eric. "You've got to love a place that parties in the streets. I was ravenous for some fun. You've been a real drag lately, my friend, with the divorce, arrest, electroshock therapy, and all the other nasty messes you've managed to get yourself into lately. I'm just saying."

"I'm sorry to disappoint you," I said. "The last few days haven't been that bad. What about the damsel in distress?"

"Well it is true I love a good rescue and fight," said Eric. "But we both know that didn't work out too well, since you had to go and get yourself shot during the rescue attempt."

"It wasn't one of my finer moments," I said. "How did you find me in the middle of this jungle…and don't tell me it's the outdoorsman in you since we both know you're a city boy to the core?"

Eric flashed a big toothy grin and then answered, "I was thinking more along the lines of badass survivalist."

"Right, when was the last time you slept on anything other than a king sized mattress?" I asked.

He curled an arm around Camo Girl's waist and said, "You mean other than the bed of leaves just last night?"

I gave him my best disgusted look.

"What are you saying?" I demanded.

"I'm saying it can get mighty cold in this jungle," he said with exaggerated innocence.

"You're not admitting to cheating on your wife, are you?" I asked.

"You have a wife?" asked Camo Girl.

"Damn right he does," I said.

She considered for an instant turning the gun on Eric, but instead, plopped her fists on her hips, pinched her brow and waited for an answer.

"Ummm, yea I do, but we have an understanding," he said.

"What kind of understanding?" she asked.

"We are…let me see," he said. How do I say this? You might say we are open-minded."

"Open-minded?" she asked.

"Yea, what do you mean…open-minded?" I asked.

"We have a don't ask don't tell policy that serves us well," he said. "Besides, after what I witnessed girl, you've got no room to complain."

Her eyes went from hard to sultry in an instant. She gave Eric a wink and added emphasis by slowly running the tip of her tongue the full circumference of her lips.

Eric gave her one of his long appraising looks before saying, "I like the way you think, girl."

His eyes were fixated on her tits, which were trying their best to escape the undersized tube top, but he spoke to me.

"Do you see, Grant?" he said. "It's like I'm always trying to tell you…no one is all bad."

"I don't know anything about a don't ask don't tell policy," I said. "You're married and I happen to care about Kinsey."

"Grant, I love you, but this is none of your business," he said. "What happens under our roof is your business. Stay out of this."

He was right of course, so I shrugged and cut my eyes to Camo Girl as a way to escape his angry stare-down.

"You hunks want to do a threesome?" asked Camo Girl. "There's something about the jungle that gets me wet as hell."

I'm pretty sure I looked exactly the way I felt…appalled. Eric busted a gut.

"Some other time, babe," said Eric. "That's not why I followed you into this God forsaken jungle."

"You followed her here?" I asked.

Eric nodded.

"Can't you think with something other than your…"

Eric interrupted before I could finish.

"Nice," he said. "You had disappeared without a trace. The only lead I had was Victor Branco, but I didn't have a clue what he looked like. I needed a plan, so I decided the only thing to do was get a drink and enjoy the carnival.

"That's a brilliant plan," I said.

Eric grinned.

"I find that I have all kinds of brilliant ideas over cocktails, don't you?" he asked.

We have this glare we use with each other when we detect bullshit. I used it on him, so Eric cut the bullshit short and continued with his story.

"I was sitting at the bar of a little hole-in-the wall enjoying an amazingly good fruity libation as the freaks paraded down the street when I noticed this chick at a nearby table looking like a total badass," said Eric.

"That would be me," said Camo Girl flashing her best badass expression.

For the first time, I realized there was a spark of mischief gleaming through Camo Girl's hard façade.

"She was talking in low tones to a dandy, who must have been in his early 40's," said Eric. "I couldn't hear any of their conversation, but she stood up, spat in his face and said loud enough for everyone in the bar to hear, "Fuck you, Victor Branco."

Eric was wearing one of those smug I told you so looks. He waited for me to tell him I thought his plan was brilliant, but I decided to hold out for more of his story first.

Eric wasn't fooled one bit by my strategy. He knew he had me, but he continued with his tale anyway.

"The guy grabbed her by the wrist and pulled her across his lap where he delivered the first of many hard slaps to her ass," he said.

I cut my eyes to Camo Girl expecting to see outrage on her face. Her eyes were indeed smoldering, but I suspect it was lust instead of outrage.

"This chick never let out a whimper," said Eric. "Instead she delivered her own brand of abuse in the form of a not stop stream of the foulest curses I've ever heard. She said unspeakable things that involved his entire family."

Eric paused for dramatic effect before continuing.

"Let me tell you, Dude, it was both shocking and a huge turn on," said Eric.

Eric pointed toward Camo Girl and shook his

head.

"She was breathing hard and I was about to step in between them and do the gentlemanly thing, when I realized she wasn't distressed at all…she was enjoying it," he said. "In fact she climaxed right there in the middle of the bar."

He shook his head in amazement.

"No one else in the bar paid a bit of attention to them," he said.. "I'm wiping the sweat from my brow as Victor lays some cash on the table and splits. All I could think was welcome to Brazil."

"You let him leave without asking about Ginny," I said.

It wasn't the first time I was completely exasperated with Eric. He was in the same room with our best lead to find Ginny and he does nothing. Instead, he let Victor leave, just like that.

"I wasn't sure whether she was a hooker or if Victor was just paying the check," said Eric. "What I did know for sure was I needed to have a conversation with this woman."

"Some conversation," said Camo Girl. "He said in a voice loud enough for half the bar to hear that he was next."

Eric flashed his trademark confident grin and said, "They don't call me Mr. Discreet for nothing."

"Does that work...telling a stranger you want them for sex?" I asked.

"When will you men ever get it through your empty heads, that women love sex as much, if not more, than you do," said Camo Girl. "Now that we earn our own money, we no longer have to pretend to be chaste just to secure a husband. Besides, who would want one...husbands make for lazy lovers. I should know. I've had four."

"Eric is someone's husband and his beautiful wife is a good friend of mine," I said to Camo Girl. "I don't get this open marriage crap, but I know one thing for sure, I don't want to see her hurt by the likes of you."

We glared at each other before Eric slapped me on the back and said, "Rest easy, my friend. I would never do anything to hurt Kinsey. I love her with all my sappy heart. Don't you want to hear what I found out about Victor?"

Damn right I wanted to hear about Victor Branco and was reminding Eric that Ginny's security chief was our best hope if we ever hoped to find her, when we heard something crashing through the forest and it was headed straight for us. It was loud and sounded big.

Camo Girl raised her gun and pointed it in the direction of the stampede. Whatever it was, it was moving fast. I dropped to a crouch in anticipation of the fight to come. Of all the things that could have burst through the foliage, the last thing I expected to see was Ginny fall face first at our feet.

I jumped between Ginny and the gun.

"Don't shoot!" I shouted.

CHAPTER 9

Ginny lay sprawled in front of us looking tired, dirty and lost. She was the most beautiful woman I had ever laid eyes on and I wanted to give her refuge…to hold her…to comfort her.

Without thinking I moved toward her, but she shrank from me. I froze. Something was wrong. She didn't seem herself. She didn't seem to see me. I looked more closely. It was more than dirt on her face; Ginny had a nasty black eye.

Concerned, I spoke her name ever so softly, but I don't think she heard me. Camo Girl brushed past me and knelt at Ginny's feet. Taking her hands, she spoke to Ginny in a soothing way. It wasn't speech so much, but more like she was humming a lullaby. A small light of recognition sparked in Ginny's eyes.

The Guardians stepped from the shadows of the jungle and formed a half circle around the two women. They began chanting, softly at first, and then more loudly in a strange ancient tongue that sounded something like Sanskrit.

My mind was running a million miles a minute. Were the Guardians chasing Ginny? Had they hurt her? I shook my head and discarded these theories before they could take root. The most likely explanation was they had just rescued her from something horrible.

The jungle began to shimmer. At first, I thought it might be the wind, but decided it was something altogether different that made the foliage around us dance ever so gracefully to the rhythm of the ancient song.

What I did know for sure was the air was filled with an electric current that drew the hair from our bodies. Not just the little hairs on our arms, but also the longer hair from our head was swaying like a snake charmer's mark.

The only time I had experienced anything like it was during a camping trip in the Red River Gorge. It was my fifth day in the backcountry and I was lying in a hammock staring out over the canyon. It was quiet and peaceful…just the break I needed from the stress of a busy law practice.

There wasn't a cloud in the sky, but I heard the rumble of distant thunder. If you've ever been camping, then you know that rain is a curse to campers. I laid there as long as I could as the wind picked up and dark clouds rolled in from the west.

Like most people, I know when to get in out of the rain. I planned to let the storm get as close as possible, before seeking shelter in my tent. When the first of the lightening tore the fabric of the sky nearby, I got a wild idea. It had been a day full of wild ideas, like sunbathing nude.

It's not like me to get naked outdoors. I had tried it once when I was five years old and was caught in the act by Ginny's mother. She so traumatized me that I swore I'd never do it again. I kept that vow for over twenty years. Still, I hadn't seen a soul in five days and figured the backcountry was empty. Besides, it was a hot day and my clothes were sticky with sweat and dirt from the trail.

The wilderness worked a strange alchemy on me. It was enough of a change that I acted on the impulse and stretched out in the sun without a stitch of clothing. I liked it enough that my clothes were still laying in a pile in the tent.

As the wind picked up, I remembered the tent wasn't staked because of the rocky ground. I imagined it lifting off and flying across the canyon, like Dorothy's little house in the Wizard of Oz.

All of my gear, including every stitch of clothing was in the tent. Damn if my hiking boots weren't in there too. I didn't want to risk losing all of my stuff, but for some strange reason, I had a compelling need to feel the rain on my naked skin.

It was twelve miles to the trailhead. I couldn't imagine hiking all that distance naked and barefooted. Even worse, what would people think when I finally made it back to civilization with bloody feet and a sunburned bare bottom.

I was torn. The sensible part of me wanted to use my body weight to anchor the tent and belongings against the force of the rising wind. The adventurous side wanted to experience the storm, naked and exposed, like a primal man.

I'm not sure how long the debate lasted because time gets weird when you're alone in the backcountry. What I know for sure is I chose the storm over my things thanks to a moment of clarity. I wasn't going to let things deprive me of this experience.

So, I stood on a rock in the middle of a huge thunder storm. The wind was blowing hard. Lightening crackled all around me. I could feel the electricity in the air as I hooted and hollered in joyous victory over the tent full of things.

I was hit by lightning that day. Thor's energy coursed through my body at the speed of light and was gone in the blink of an eye. All that was left was the metallic taste of cold steel and a completely different view of life and death.

The Guardian's mystical chant filled the air with the taste of cold steel. Steam rose from our skin and enveloped us in a foggy cloud.

The chant descended along the same path it rose. It slowed and softened, first to a whisper, and then to silence. When it was over, Ginny found her way back to the here and now. This simple act somehow pulled her from the dark place she was in.

At first, she looked bewildered, as if she couldn't imagine how she came to be in this place. Then her eyes found me.

Her lips moved. It was only a whisper.

"Grant, is that really you?" she asked.

Just as I was about to throw my arms around her someone grabbed my right wrist and yanked hard. Instinctively, I countered with an arm bar. Slamming him roughly to the ground, I jammed a knee into his lower back and pinned him face first into the dirt.

Ginny let out a yelp.

"No, Grant," she said.

I looked at her and then back at the man on the ground. For the first time, I got a good look at his face and let out a gasp. It was Pony Tail.

Since this crazy adventure began, Pony Tail had appeared at key moments...usually when something bad was about to happen. I didn't like the site of him one bit. Of course, my intense dislike for him might also have something to do with seeing him behave so intimately toward Ginny a few days earlier.

Then there was the shooting at the Center. He pulled a handgun from his pants and tried to kill us. Damn if he didn't hit me with one of those shots, but I was lucky enough to escape with only a scratch.

Yep, I would say I had some pretty damn good reasons to dislike this guy, but I also had to admit there were a few things about him that didn't add up. Like for instance, there was this business about him being a healer. He might have saved Uncle Jim's life.

Come to think of it, I found him hovering over Ginny in the hospital and now she was protecting him. I didn't like this one bit, but was about to do as she asked and let him up, when I realized there couldn't be a plausible reason why he was here in this remote part of the Amazon Rainforest with Ginny, so I shifted tactics.

"Who are you?" I growled.

He didn't answer. I waited. Just when I thought it would never come, I noticed he had a clump of dirt jammed into his mouth. It's possible he couldn't speak because I had his face pinned to the Earth.

I thought about giving him room to spit out the dirt, but a part of me wasn't willing to be reasonable. I took pleasure in knowing I was in total control, and if I was honest with myself, I also wanted to punish him for all of the trespasses I was sure he had committed against me.

Ginny had other ideas.

"Please, let him up Grant," she said.

I wanted to give her whatever she asked for…to never say no to her, but feeling that way about someone was new to me, and must admit, it was causing some discomfort. For now, I had issues with her request.

"This guy tried to kill us," I said.

Unbelievably, Ginny shook her head. She was there for God's sake. I have a tendency to get a little stressed when I'm torn between something I really want and something I fear.

So I added in a voice that was too whiney for my satisfaction, "He shot me at the Center, Ginny."

In a tone of voice we usually reserve for the severely impaired, Ginny said, "If you let my brother up and give him a chance to spit that clump of dirt out of his mouth, then maybe he could explain to you what really happened at the Center."

Pony Tail is Ginny's brother! I couldn't believe it. I tried to think, but my head was spinning.

Finally, I hissed, "That's impossible. He's an assassin."

"My brother is not an assassin," she said. "He

was protecting me."

"What do you mean protecting you?" I asked.

Ginny said, "Let him up. We will explain everything."

I didn't move.

She tried again, "Grant, my father sent him."

Ginny's father was dead and it was time for her to face reality.

"I know you want to believe he is still alive, Ginny, but your father is gone and you have no siblings," I said.

Ginny glared at me, and then puffed out her chest, as if she planned to give me a blast of shit that would blow me half way back to Kentucky, but it didn't come. Instead her eyes shifted to something over my shoulder and every drop of blood seemed to drain from her face.

I couldn't imagine what it might be, but I sure didn't expect to hear a deep voice say, "It's okay, Grant, you're both here now."

The voice was vaguely familiar. I sifted through millions of bits of information in an instant before it hit me. Turning slowly I fixed my gaze on the big Viking.

His eyes were wet and shinning. One by one, the stream of tears made their way down the line of his nose, then curving along his upper lip and finally changing direction to make the turn around the corner of the mouth before dripping to the soil at his feet.

Ginny stood transfixed before him, a ghost made flesh. Neither spoke for a time. It was Ginny who broke the silence.

"Daddy…is that you?" asked Ginny.

The big Viking nodded and opened his arms to embrace her.

"Yes, Lil Froggy," he said.

"Oh my God, it is you," she said.

There was no hesitation left. Ginny rushed into his arms and held him tight. It was her turn to sob, and sob she did.

I crouched awkwardly on Pony Tail for another half second before getting up and pulling him to his feet. We glared at each other as he spit out the clod of dirt and wiped his mouth with the back of his hand. When he was finished, he pushed past me to join Ginny and her dad in a group cry-hug.

CHAPTER 10

The hike back to the village was slower and more relaxed than earlier. No one seemed concerned that nightfall was coming to the jungle. I was relieved we found Ginny, but was also worried about her. She was convinced she had found her father, but I didn't believe it was him. None of this was adding up.

I wanted to talk some sense into her, but she stayed close to him, cheerfully chattering non-stop about her life since his disappearance twenty years earlier. I didn't get a sense he was a bad guy. In fact, much like the rest of the villagers, he seemed to be a decent human being.

Still, there is no way in hell he could possibly be her father. Ginny's father would be a middle-aged man by now. Instead the Viking looked like he was our age. I wasn't ready to accept that this twenty-something man could possibly be her father. It defied logic.

To complicate matters, it wasn't just him. All of the Guardians looked to be twenty-something and that isn't the only odd thing about them. They claim to guard the gateway to paradise. I'm not sure what they mean by that, but the one thing I could say for certain about them is they are the most pleasant group of people I've ever had the pleasure of knowing.

"Why so quiet, Dude?" asked Eric.

In response, I showed him the most exaggerated glum face I could muster. Eric flashed teeth bleached so white they look fake. When he spoke again, it was with exaggerated cheerfulness.

"Where's the happy-go-lucky guy we all know and love?" asked Eric.

I nodded toward Mr. Viking and asked, "Do you believe this guy is really her father?"

Eric pinched his brow and then told Camo Girl to follow the rest of the group. Once she was gone, he grabbed my upper arm and pulled me to the side to give the Guardians behind us room to pass.

When the last of them was out of site, he asked, "Have you forgotten, Grant?"

At first, I didn't have a clue what he meant, but then it came in a flash. When we were kids running the streets barefooted, we sometimes pretended we were Indian trackers. We got very good at moving undetected around the neighborhood and made a game of sneaking up on people.

We saw some things we shouldn't have seen.

Like Mrs. Sims kissing the cable guy. Later we saw her husband sobbing alone in the garage. Embarrassed for him, we tiptoed away without a sound. The next day, we were stunned to hear he passed away from a mysterious illness. That was the official G-rated story for us kids, but we overheard the real story. Mr. Sims stuffed a potato in the tail pipe of his car and closed the garage door.

Of course the Sims tragedy isn't what Eric was asking me to remember. No, we saw other things during our forays into the wilds of suburban Louisville and one of those things is relevant to this story.

One evening, as the sun touched the horizon, we saw Ginny's parents arguing in the fading light. They were an odd couple. She was dark, short, and fat. He was tall, fit, and very blond. The top of her head just barely reached his chest. More importantly, she was mean spirited and fought dirty, while he was calm and reasonable.

"What kind of man are you?" asked Ginny's mom.

"I'm the kind of man who does the right thing," he said.

"You've lost your mind, Bill," she said sarcastically.

"Maria, try to understand, this is necessary," he said.

"It's not necessary for you to leave your family on some fool's mission," she said.

"I have to go back to Brazil," he said. "There's too much at stake."

"Do you really think some jungle weed is going to make a difference?" asked Maria.

"There may be no limit to what it will cure," he said. "It could make the world a better place."

"The world can go fuck itself," growled Maria. "All I care about is my family."

"You can't be that selfish," said Bill.

Maria jabbed her husband in the chest with a stiff finger and said, "You heard those FBI people."

Bill shook his head, "How can a healing plant be a dangerous narcotic?"

"If the government says it's bad, like heroin, then we don't want anything to do with it," she said.

"That shaman cured me with it," he said. "It's nothing like heroin. It's not destructive at all. It feels wholesome, like perfect health."

She rolled her eyes and said, "Perfect health my ass. Bill, just tell them everything."

Ginny's father shook his head.

"If I do, then they don't need us anymore," he said. "There is a lot at stake, Maria. These people are capable of anything."

"Find another way," she pleaded. "Don't go

back to that damn jungle."

He ran his hand through his hair and said, "There's no other way."

"Don't leave us here alone," she said.

With a heavy sigh he said, "I'm going. For all of our sakes, I'm going and it's too dangerous to take you along."

She stomped off to the house and slammed the door behind her.

The last thing I heard her say was, "Go to hell then."

As we slipped away I remember thinking Ginny's dad looked so sad. I didn't like her mother one bit. Of course, that wasn't the first time I had seen her red faced and angry.

Yes, we had seen some things while skulking around the neighborhood like little cold war spies.

"Eric, I remember what Ginny's dad said, but we both know if he was alive, he'd be a middle aged man by now," I said.

"I know it defies logic, but you need to open your mind," said Eric. "If not your mind, then at least open your eyes. You'd have to be blind to not see that he is her father."

In response, I clinched my jaw and glared at him. Eric shook his head sadly.

"Dude, you've been a real drag lately," said Eric. "Sometimes you act like a little old woman.

I'm just saying."

I knew he was right. I had plenty of excuses for my behavior, but excuses are the mainstay of failures and I sure as hell wasn't ready to include myself in that group. I had been off balance lately thanks to a series of events that challenged my assumptions. It was time to pull myself together.

That's exactly when Pony Tail slipped up so quietly it startled me. It bothered me that I wasn't paying better attention to my surroundings. I had been trained better than that, but then again, maybe there was a reason for it. Ch'ing once told me we stumble from time to time for no apparent reason other than to keep us humble.

"I don't really like guns much," he said

I figured he was bullshitting me since he shot me a few days ago. Or, had it been longer than that. I had one of those weird moments, when time gets all fuzzy. I couldn't say for sure how long it had been since he shot me, since I didn't know how long they had kept me drugged in the loony bin.

I tried my best to shake off the time warp and said, "Maybe you should have thought of that before you pulled a gun on me."

He shrugged.

"I saved your life," said Pony Tail.

I shook my head.

"You tried to kill me," I said.

Pony Tail slid his index finger across his throat with a dramatic flourish.

"You were about to get your throat slit," he said.

I swallowed hard. It was purely a reflex action, but I hated to show weakness to this guy. I tried to deflect attention from it by using my best tough guy voice.

"What are you saying?" I demanded.

The tough guy act didn't work. My voice raised an octave, rather than drop one, like I intended. To his credit he noticed it, but instead of taking advantage, he softened his tone a bit more. The guy was trying to put me at ease.

"I saw a someone behind you with a knife," he said. "Scorned lover, maybe?"

"Impossible," I said.

Pony Tail raised an eyebrow. The scorned lover comment was ridiculous, but he may be right about the rest of it. I had forgotten that I sensed someone behind me and was about to turn around when he pulled the gun and the shooting started. It occurred to me he might be telling the truth, but I had more questions.

"What were you doing back stage?" I asked.

"We had information that they were going to make a move for my sister," he said. "I was there to protect her."

"Ginny?" I asked.

He nodded.

"Who were you protecting her from?" I asked.

"Much will be revealed very soon," interrupted Layah. "Come, we are almost there."

"None of this makes a bit of sense," I grumbled.

She gave me a gentle pat on the shoulder and said, "Patience Grasshopper."

The reference to my favorite classic television show was a surprise. Under other circumstances it may have felt dismissive, but Layah's face was filled with kindness.

"We're not far now," she said.

"Come on, Dude," said Eric. "When all else fails, follow the naked babe."

"It always comes back to that," I said with a shake of the head.

Eric stopped in his tracks, folded his arms across his chest, and with the most offended expression he could muster said, "Such disrespect…and coming from the hypocrite who has seen fit to liberate his boys from underwear prison, no less."

Somehow I'd forgotten I was naked. In this place it seemed natural, like the Garden of Eden before the fall. I had been such a prude before and was pondering this huge change when we broke through the dense foliage and stepped into a small village.

"Yeah, I guess I've gone native," I said.

Eric slapped me on the back and said, "It's about time, my friend."

He didn't wait for a response, but instead called out to Camo Girl, who had been flirting outrageously with Teekal, to come explore this cool place with him. They split together without another word.

I thought it would be a good time to talk to Ginny, and found her near the central fire chatting with Layah. As I approached, I couldn't help but notice her eyes were focused below the waist. In the face of her frank appraisal, my newfound casualness about nudity suddenly evaporated. I was exposed to her once again.

It was useless to wish for clothes, but I wished for them anyway and couldn't seem to stop myself from looking anywhere but directly at her. When it became too much, I let it go and gave her my undivided attention.

The hunger in Ginny's eyes was a huge turn on. Her breath caught in her throat when my body responded in a predictable way. Getting turned-on in public was way beyond my comfort level, but I didn't know how to stop it.

"Well, aren't you full of surprises," said Ginny in a husky voice.

I wanted her, but I didn't want to show it to everybody. Desperately I searched for a way out, a safe retreat, but the glow in her eyes pulled me forward, toward her.

"Ginny…" I said, but then again, it may have been just a croak. It's hard to say for sure.

She began speaking at the same time, but left me standing there stunned when her eyes rolled back and she collapsed midway through the first syllable. Layah didn't miss a beat and took charge, sounding an awful lot like an emergency room nurse.

"Ginny needs rest and medicine," said Layah.

I snapped out of the trance I was in and gathered her in my arms. Layah pointed to one of the shelters, where I laid her in a bed of red and yellow feathers.

They stripped her clothes and someone fed them to the fire. Teekal applied a paste to her wounds and then they covered her with a soft blanket with a subtle design woven into the fabric. It depicted a snake swallowing a bird's tail and the bird swallowing the snake's tail.

When she briefly regained consciousness, she was given a few sips from a delicate bowl that appeared to be carved from rosewood. There were faint markings on the rim that I resolved to check out at the first opportunity, but for now, I was concerned with Ginny's recovery.

I hovered around her feeling scared and helpless. Her sleep was restless. Each time she awoke briefly from her rest, she was given another sip from the bowl.

I stayed with her all day and through the night. At one point or another, I think all of the Guardians looked in on her, but the Viking and Pony Tail stayed the longest. Finally, she rested peacefully.

By morning, the black eye and the sores were gone. I was relieved she looked like herself again. I can't say the same for myself. When she finally awoke, I was at her side.

"How do you feel Ginny?" I asked.

"I feel great, but you look like hell, Grant," she answered.

I nodded and asked, "What happened to you?"

Ginny searched my face for a moment before she said, "After Dr. Wiemp gave you the sedative, they quickly loaded you onto a gurney and rolled it away. I started to follow, but got a call from one of my investigators. She had information that my father was alive and being held captive by a group of dangerous radicals. There wasn't much time and I needed to get on a flight as soon as possible."

"You left me," I said.

"I felt bad about that," she said. "I kept telling myself you were in good hands, but I knew that was a lie so I called Uncle Jim and told him where you were."

"How did you get away from Dr. Wiemp and his goons?" I asked.

"Everyone was focused on you," she answered. "I moved away from the noise to better hear the phone. When the call was over, I found that I had wandered around the corner and was standing in front of the elevator. The door opened, I got on it, and never looked back."

I opened my mouth to ask her a question, but she quickly added, "I'm sorry I ditched you, Grant. There is no good excuse."

"I guess we're even," I said.

When we were kids, Ginny's mother caught us with our pants down. We weren't doing anything other than being curious about the differences between boys and girls, but her mother had an intense reaction. Under threat of force, she made me promise to never speak to Ginny again.

It was the hardest thing I ever had to do. Ginny was my best friend, and I loved her as only a five year old can, but I kept the promise. It cost me in ways I could never have predicted, since the fear and lost landed me in Sadistic Doctor's hateful hands.

Wiping a tear from her cheek, Ginny said, "It had nothing to do with our past. Finding my father has been a lifetime obsession."

"Of course it didn't," I said. "I'm sorry I brought it up. That's a long time to keep searching for a missing person. What made you think he was alive all these years?"

Ginny chewed on her lower lip as she thought about her answer. It was something I had seen her do as a child many times.

"I am connected to my father," she said. "Maybe it's because of my mother's illness. I'm not sure. What I do know for sure is I could feel him…feel his life force, if you will. He was…is still alive. I knew this with an absolute certainty, even when everyone else had given up."

"This man you met today…he's our age Ginny," I said. "Your father would be a middle aged man right now."

Ginny's eyes flashed angry then softened.

"I know it's weird," she said. "I don't understand it, but he is my father," she said.

It was time for a graceful retreat, so I asked, "How did you end up deep in the jungle, injured and alone?"

"I was abducted," she said.

"Was it Slotter?" I asked.

She shook her head.

"Who then?" I asked.

She shrugged.

"Any theories?" I asked.

"I have a few ideas, but who knows if I'm

right," she answered.

"What are they?" I asked.

"My company is committed to social reform in Latin America and I've made some enemies," she said.

"I thought you sold designer clothing to rich people," I said.

"We do, but unlike our competitors, our clothes are not manufactured in third world sweatshops," said Ginny.

"What are you trying to reform?" I asked.

"Our focus is on Latin women," she said. "They are treated like property here."

I nodded my head in agreement.

"I was reading about the slave trade on the flight over," I said. "It is disturbing."

"The problem is deep-seated," she said. "South America's machismo culture is male orientated and women are expected to submit to their will and whim. Many are slaves, but even in the best case scenario, they are hardly more than servants to be used by the men in their lives."

"So how do you plan to change these attitudes?" I asked.

"Part of the problem is economics," answered Ginny. "Men control the money and women are financially dependent on them for survival. This gives the men too much power over their lives. I give them good paying jobs so these women have money of their own."

"I can see where having their own money would be a game changer," I said. "Still, it sounds to me like these are the kind of men who would just take it away from them."

"Sometimes they do," she said. "This isn't an easy or overnight process. It takes time. Attitudes must change, so I also train them to be decision makers and managers. Slowly, they are learning how to be in charge of their own lives."

I thought about Ch'ing's teachings on living an authentic life. We come into this world fresh and free, but it doesn't take long for well-meaning people to bully us into conformity.

Each time we concede, we abdicate a little more of our sovereignty. Eventually, we become so disempowered we are little more than slaves. The Taoist path offers one way to reverse this process and live a self-directed life where we are our own masters.

"That sounds like practical Taoism to me," I said.

"I don't know much about Taoism," said Ginny. "For me, Ch'ing was just a sweet guy who taught you boys martial arts. I was more influenced by Marguerite's teaching. Nature was her classroom. We looked at what folks would call Mother Nature and we also looked inside at our own nature. The aim was to live an authentic life. She emphasized things like living independently in a co-dependent world."

"That could also sum up the heart of Ch'ing's teachings," I said. "People like to talk about freedom, but when push comes to shove, they follow the herd. He encouraged us to resist the herd instinct."

"Some follow, while others fight to maintain control over the followers," said Ginny.

"I bet there are some who don't support your efforts to help Hispanic women become more independent and self-reliant," I said.

"There are a group of angry men who think these reforms are the devil's work," said Ginny.

"You think they are behind this?" I asked.

"I don't know for sure, but my instincts tell me they are," she answered.

"Why don't you tell me what happened," I said.

She nodded and began her story.

"After getting the call about my father, I went straight to the hotel where I quickly packed a bag and headed to the airport" said Ginny. "I got as far as the parking garage when I heard footsteps behind me. For some reason it made me nervous, so I picked the pace up, but whoever was behind me broke into a run. I panicked and turned to face the stalker, but all I saw was a fist. The creep punched me hard in the face."

Without thinking I reached out and touched the spot on her face where a nasty bruise had been just a few hours earlier.

"The blow knocked me out cold," said Ginny. "When I awoke I was laying on my side. I tried to roll over to get circulation back into my arm, but thumped my knee. There was little room to move. To make matters worse, I had a pounding headache."

"It was pitch black," said Ginny. "I didn't have a clue where I was or how I got there. I heard a familiar sound, but couldn't quite place it at first. It took a minute to figure out it was road noise. I was in the trunk of a car and it was hot."

"It was several hours before we stopped," said Ginny. "I could hear the car door open and then gas flowing into the tank. I started yelling and pounding on the inside of the trunk. No one seemed to hear me."

"We stopped many more times, but the trunk was never opened," continued Ginny. "I had no idea whether it was night or day. I fell in and out of a restless sleep. Time disappeared. I could no longer feel my arms and legs. My clothes were soaked with sweat. The trunk stank of urine and motor oil. Hope slipped away."

"When light finally poured back into the trunk, I was barely conscious," said Ginny. Someone pulled me out and dropped me to the ground. I heard voices but couldn't comprehend what was being said. The language was familiar, but the words just jumbled in my head."

Ginny paused for a breath and to gather her thoughts before returning to the narrative. She crinkled her nose, looked at me and then shook it off.

"I smelled something like a burnt match and opened my eyes," said Ginny. "A gruesome face contorted with hate leered at me. Why are you doing this, I asked. The bastard sneered and told me I was about to learn my value. He said I was too old to get top price, but he should be able to sell me to one of the lesser whore houses for a few pesos."

Ginny shivered slightly and again paused in the telling of her story. Before she resumed, I saw something flash across her face that looked to me like a moment of realization.

"You don't have to do this," I said gently.

She gave me a sad little smile and went on with her story anyway.

"The thought of being a sex slave in a third world brothel was not my idea of a good time," said Ginny. "I laid there shivering in the dirt, wishing I could just die. I didn't see any way out."

"It was then I heard another voice," said Ginny. "It was a much kinder voice that whispered to me. It told me to be brave, because help was on the way."

"At first I thought the voice was only in my head," said Ginny. "I figured it was like a mirage, or something, but he told me he was real. When he said to look to the right, I saw him standing there with a three toed sloth draped across his shoulders. I could be wrong, but they looked like they had been smoking some really good weed. Their kind faces were filled with sparkling eyes and shit-eating grins. Strangely, it filled me with hope. "

"The sloth wasn't the only odd thing about him," said Ginny. "He was naked except for a shiny gold medallion around his neck. The medallion looked oddly familiar. It depicted a snake eating a bird and the bird simultaneously eating the snake. His lips never moved, but I distinctly heard him tell me not to worry. Then I blacked out."

"When I recovered consciousness, I was bouncing in the back of a pickup truck," said Ginny. "I have to tell you, it was a huge relief to be out of the trunk. I was beginning to think things might be looking up, when I saw a flash of lightening and heard the rumble of thunder. The sky opened and the rain came hard. The temperature dropped. I was cold and miserable. The only upside came when I opened my mouth and got a few drops of water to drink."

"When the rain finally stopped, the sun came out with a vengeance," said Ginny. "I tried to position myself to minimize exposure, but there was only one way I could lay without irritating the sores spots. I was pretty sure they were infected. Despite the brutal heat, I was cold and shivering. I knew I was running a high fever. On the positive side, I figured I'd be long dead before we made it to the brothels and that was oddly comforting."

"I don't know how many days we traveled through swamp land and forest," said Ginny. "The road was rough, barely a trail. When we got stuck in the mud, Match Breath first checked the ropes that bound my hands and feet, and then left me in the bed of the truck while he walked off."

"I figured he went to get others. It was the first time I was left alone and I didn't want to waste it. I needed to find a way to escape, but first I had to find a way to cut the ropes. I had limited mobility and couldn't see what he had tied me to. I tried to feel it, but that didn't work either."

"I didn't know how much time I had and every second was vital. Fighting back a wave of panic, I chose to replace it with a sense of urgency instead. I took a deep calming breath and saw the solution right in front of me."

"At each of the four corners of the truck bed was a metal eye-hook. The edges looked sharp enough to cut the rope if I worked it back and forth long enough. I figured it would be a slow process, but it was my only chance. I said a little prayer of gratitude and got started."

"I didn't know if it was a good plan or not, but it was all I had. I started with enthusiasm, but my resolve was challenged when the ropes didn't cut easily. Several hours later I was still trying to cut the rope and on the verge of giving up, but the fear of being a sex slave kept me going. My hopes were dashed when Match Breath returned hours later and I was still tied to the truck."

"He had brought several more men with him, two teenage boys and an old man. The boys acted shy and didn't look at me. The old man was a different matter. As they pushed the truck out of the mud, I showed him the ropes."

"Even though the old man was taller than Match Breath, he lowered himself to the smaller man's level and asked what I was doing tied to the back of his truck. Match Breath raised his chin and sneered. The old man rose to his full height, but I'll never know what he intended to say because Match Breath pulled a pistol from his pocket and shot the old man in the chest."

"The boys left the old man bleeding next to a

mud hole and fled into the forest. Match Breath calmly started the truck and drove off at a leisurely pace."

"Then the terrain changed from swampland and became more mountainous. The truck started up a steep hill and I slid to the back slamming against the tailgate. It clanged open and I rolled out the back. I expected the truck to stop but it didn't. Instead, it ground its way up and over the hill. I rolled myself into the bushes and waited. I expected to hear the truck stop and the asshole come looking for me, but it never happened."

"After a while, I started laughing. It was hesitant at first, but quickly overwhelmed me until it bordered on hysteria. That's when it turned to tears…gut wrenching tears."

"When the last of the sobs subsided, I took stock of my situation. I had a bruised shoulder from the fall, but I was alive. All of the hard work on the ropes had finally paid off and the bindings around my wrist gave way to the weight of my body on the uphill grade. I fumbled with the remaining rope around my ankles."

"Once my feet were free, I took a moment to rub circulation into my joints. My biggest concern was the possibility Match Breath would return for me. I had to move deeper into the jungle to be safe. I was also lost. I could wander aimlessly in the forest or I could head back into the swamp and try to find those boys. I imagined snakes and other foul creatures in the swamp. There had to be another alternative. I heard running water and thirst made my decision for me."

"My legs were weak, but I managed to hobble in the direction of the stream. The water was surprisingly cool and crystal clear. After a long drink, I stripped my clothes and let the stream wash away the ordeal. It might have been the best bath I've ever taken. Even though I knew the nightmare wasn't over, I finally had a chance."

"After resting, I decided to follow the stream. I knew it would empty into a larger river where there was a greater likelihood I would find help. After going so long without water, I also wanted to stay close to a source."

"It was good to move again. Regardless of the outcome, I was once again in control of my own destiny."

"As I maneuvered through the thick vegetation, my mind wandered. After all of my effort to protect the rainforest, it was odd that it now threatened me. Lost in thought, I failed to pay close attention to my surroundings. When I heard voices, I dropped to a crouch and peered through the foliage."

"It was Match Breath again. He wasn't alone this time. He and another man were moving in my direction. The new guy had a snake tattooed on his right arm. His face was hard and cruel. He stopped and sniffed the air. His eyes narrowed and he pointed in my direction. Shit. I was screwed again. What now, I wondered?"

"I was about to run, when a man with a blond ponytail appeared out of nowhere. He hit Match Breath hard in the mouth with his left hand, while he simultaneously sliced the other guy's throat with a commando knife held in the other. Despite the hard blow, Match Breath recovered enough to make a grab for the knife, but it was quickly buried deep in his gut. Both men crumbled to the ground."

"It was over in an instant. I didn't know whether I should cheer or run for my life, so I ran. I ran even though I had a nagging feeling I had seen that distinctive blond ponytail somewhere before. The last words I heard before I disappeared into the bush was, I'm your brother."

CHAPTER 11

I had a thousand and one questions for Ginny, but it had been a long sleepless night. Exhaustion finally had her way with me and I closed my eyes a couple of hours before dawn. The story of Ginny's harrowing car trip south of the equator wove its way through my dreams and yet I still slept soundly knowing she was safe.

When I finally opened them again to a new day, Ginny was bent close whispering something in my ear that I couldn't quite make out. Layah stood behind her with a leather bound book held high over her head. The morning sun peaked above the book like lady liberty's torch lighting the way for all seeking a new life in the land of the free and home of the brave.

Ignoring the book, Ginny said to Layah, "I'd like to see my father now."

"Soon," said Layah. "Ginny, this journal was kept by your father and he asked me to give it to you. It will explain much."

"Thank you, but why doesn't he just give it to me himself," said Ginny.

"He wanted to, but was called away on

assignment," said Layah.

Ginny pressed her lips together, but a small hiss escaped all the same. She looked pretty damn pissed to me and I thought she might say something harsh to Layah, but she somehow managed to keep her disappointment in check.

"After all this time, I hoped we would have some time together," said Ginny in a tight voice.

"Please don't be too disappointed in him," said Layah in soothing tone. "It is a mission critical task that couldn't wait."

With furrowed brow, Ginny muttered, "Mission…humph," but she said nothing more.

"You must have a lot of questions for him," said Layah. "The journal will answer many of them. Afterwards, I will fill in as many gaps as I can. The rest will have to wait for your father's return."

Ginny absent mindedly stroked the book as she considered it. She took a deep breath and released the tension held in her shoulders. The hard expression softened as her curiosity replaced disappointment.

She opened her father's diary to the first page and read the inscription in a voice that was almost a whisper, "To my beloved Ginny, on this her 9th birthday."

Ginny managed to choke back a sob, but she couldn't prevent her eyes from filling with tears.

It took a few minutes, but she finally bowed her head and began reading. I imagined she was searching for answers to all of her questions.

I'm not sure how much time passed before the others left for the hot spring. I declined their invitation, content to stay and watch Ginny read.

She never once looked up from the book and I waited, quiet as a church mouse, for her to finish. It gave me time to reflect on all she had been through. Her ordeal revealed much about her character. She was truly something special and I felt privileged to know her.

I must have dozed off, because when I opened my eyes again, Ginny was sitting at my feet. Her expression was complex. On the one hand, there was an air of serenity I had never seen in her face. On the other, she seemed dangerous, as if she was coiled for a strike. Without speaking, she handed me her father's journal. Curious, I opened the book to the first page and began to read.

* * *

My Little Froggy, I miss you very much and wish with all my heart I could be with you. I am setting pen to paper so you will know it is no small matter that keeps me from you. Once you have read this account, you will understand that I have stayed in this remote place, not for selfish reasons of my own, but instead, to protect you.

To begin, I want you to know that this story is so incredible that I have decided it would be best if I tell it as it happened and avoid any commentary that might taint its objective telling.

The world is full of suffering. When I entered the job market after college, I wanted to have a positive impact on people's lives. I believed beyond a shadow of doubt that I was destined to eradicate human suffering. So, I took a position as a research scientist with the world's largest pharmaceutical company, Pathogen.

Little did I know, I had stepped onto a stage at the center of a great drama that will thrust us all into a whirlwind of change. Perhaps it's best I didn't know, because I may have faltered at the starting gate if I had even a glimpse of where it would lead and the personal price I would pay.

I hadn't been with the company long before I was assigned to a team of scientists searching for the cure of a dreadful virus. A few weeks earlier, a team of explorers from National Geographic found the doors to a cold war era Soviet laboratory standing wide open. In the wake of budgetary cuts, security personnel had been re-assigned and looters ransacked the unguarded building.

It was believed that the facility was used by the

Soviets to develop bio-weapons during the cold war, but of course the Russian government vehemently denied it. We were told the Soviets used the lab to develop a virus called "Deathblow." When exposed to the virus, our lab rats died a painful death within minutes of exposure. It was horrible.

Intelligence sources reported the virus had fallen into the hands of radical terrorist groups. It was our mission to find a cure before it was used as a weapon against innocent people. We were in a race against time and worked around the clock to find a vaccine.

Our search for a treatment frustrated us. We failed many times and were close to giving up hope. If it wasn't for Pathogen's CEO, Wilbur Goth, we would have quit many times. He is the most determined man I have ever known. Each time we tried to give up, he told us to keep looking because there's a cure for everything. I was proud to model my life after him.

Unlike Goth, we had little faith. In the end, his spirited pep talks didn't last long. When we were certain all hope was lost, something horrible happened in the lab. There was an accident that exposed us to the virus. I watched all of my co-workers die. I was the lone survivor.

Goth was outraged that we breached protocol. When he finally calmed down, he sent in a team outfitted with hazmat suits, to scan everything in the lab, including me. We needed to know why I was unaffected by the deadly virus, so they turned me into a human guinea pig.

I endured months of fruitless poking and testing. Every theory, no matter how wild it seemed, was considered. We followed every lead, but all were dead ends. The virus defeated us at every turn.

Through all the frustrating moments, the thing that bothered me the most was the nagging feeling I already knew the answer. It seemed to hover near me like a ghost that refused to abandon the mortal world. The answer was close at hand, yet remained elusive. It was maddening.

The breakthrough came from an unexpected source. A giant sinkhole suddenly appeared in Guatemala City, gobbling up most of a city block. Video taken from the air showed a bottomless black hole leading to some unknown Hell. I was astounded that it was a perfect circle and there appeared to be drill marks in the granite.

The news reporter read a script about the natural process that causes sink holes, but she didn't look convinced. Neither was I. The hole didn't look natural at all. It looked to me like a giant shaft had been drilled by some ancient technology and then covered up until years of rainfall once again exposed it to the world.

There was something else about it that caught my attention. I only caught a glimpse of it, but I'm certain I saw marks in the stone just before it flashed off the television.

I rushed to my computer and searched online for pictures of the sinkhole. None of them gave me a clear view of the markings, but I could see enough to confirm it wasn't my imagination. Etched in the stone was an ancient symbol similar to an Ouroboros, but instead of a snake swallowing its own tail, it depicted a snake eating a bird, and the bird simultaneously eating the snake.

The picture stirred a memory from our honeymoon. Your mother and I took a cruise down the Amazon River with nothing but the gear we could stuff into a couple of backpacks. I know it's an unusual honeymoon location, but I was drawn by some inexplicable force to the Amazon River.

At first, the boat ride sounded like an amazingly romantic adventure, but the trip did not go well. While on the river, I became ill. In desperation, your mother sought help from a lone native standing on the river bank. In the throes of fever, I saw only his kind eyes and a gold medallion around his neck. The medallion depicted a snake eating a bird, and the bird simultaneously eating the snake.

The man gave me a few sips of an herbal tea and told me to rest. As far as we could tell, there wasn't another person within miles of this location, let alone a hospital. Your mother figured I was as good as dead, but during the night the fever broke. The next day there wasn't a sore bone in my body.

What a miracle! In the middle of nowhere, we had the good fortune to stumble upon a Medicine Man, who was gracious enough to heal me. When I asked him about the medicinal tea he gave me the night before, he handed me a leaf.

"This is Great Mother," said the Medicine Man. "When darkness rides the four winds, you will return."

I figured something was lost in the translation, but I was grateful all the same. When we returned to Louisville, I stuck the leaf in a book and forgot about it. I had a new wife, a family to start, and a deadly virus to cure. I believed in science and for the next few years I was consumed with the search for a cure.

I had all but forgotten the leaf until I saw the sink hole and the carving of the snake eating bird. It reminded me of the Medicine Man's medallion and his magical cure, Great Mother.

Years later, sitting in the comfort of my own home, it seemed incredible that the sinkhole in Guatemala City could have the same strange snake eating bird symbol as the Shaman's gold medallion. I took a few minutes to ponder what it meant. Could there be some connection between the two, I wondered. If there was, I sure didn't see it.

It had been several years and I wasn't sure which book I stuck the leaf in or if I even still owned the book, but it was worth a try. As I stood in my library staring at the shelves of books, there was one that stood out above all others. I leaned a little closer and read the title on the spine. It was the classic Jules Verne book, "Journey to the Center of the Earth."

I first opened Verne's book one rainy day many years ago and learned the power of story. I could barely read at the time. In fact, like most school children, I found reading to be a tortuous affair and never imagined it could bring me pleasure. Journey to the Center of the Earth took the younger me on a magic carpet ride to a wondrous place deep inside of the Earth.

Verne stirred my imagination in ways I didn't know were possible. When I opened his book, it returned the favor by opening my mind to possibilities I never knew existed. I dreamed I would someday uncover life's mysteries.

In fact, that's why I decided to be a scientist. Science is a systematic tool for discovery and I wanted to be a discoverer when I grew up. Many years later, the sight of the old tome still stirred visions of prehistoric creatures living inside the hollow Earth. Verne's book truly held a special place in my heart.

So, it was with a trembling hand, that I reached out and took the dusty old hardback from the shelf. I didn't open it immediately. Instead, I held it in my hands and felt the weight of it. For something so light, it carried an unbelievable amount of what I like to call, "idea-weight".

I raised it to my nose and inhaled deeply. I love the smell of old books. If infinite possibilities had a smell, I imagine it would be the scent of a book. I'm not sure how long I stood there with the tip of my nose pressed against the book's cover, but when I finally returned to the present, I couldn't tell which world was more real…the library den on the Earth's firm surface or the prehistoric jungle at the center of the Earth. Imagination is a wondrous thing.

The book seemed to open itself and what I found astounded me. Buried between its pages was the leaf and it was as fresh as the day the Medicine Man handed it to me. As I pondered this great mystery, a phrase from Verne's book jumped off the page, "While there is life there is hope."

The next morning I rushed into my supervisor's office and excitedly told him the

Amazon story. He was not impressed, but did take the leaf, and rather absentmindedly, mumbled something about looking into it. Months went by without a word. Each time I asked him about it, he just shrugged and told me to get back to work.

Then one day after work, two men showed up at our house. They quickly flashed identification and claimed to be Federal Agents. We were told they had a search warrant and watched helplessly as they tore our home apart.

A few personal papers and the computer were the only things they found of interest. At first we didn't know what they were looking for, but when they began questioning us about the dangerous narcotic we brought back from the Rainforest, we knew this intrusion had to do with the Shaman's leaf.

The Feds questioned us for several hours about the leaf. They wanted to know where we got it and whether we had any more. We told them the Amazon story and assured them the one leaf was all we had.

They threatened to lock us away in prison if we didn't cooperate with them. The thing is, we were cooperating and I sure didn't believe the leaf was dangerous. There was something wholesome about the Shaman's tea. I felt the goodness of it from the very first sip and there was no doubt in my mind that it cured me.

I was beginning to smell a rat, but your mother was beside herself. She begged the agents to show us mercy. She frantically tried to convince them the Shaman was just a silly old man who called the leaf "Great Mother." What a silly name for a plant she pleaded. How could we possibly know it was a dangerous drug, she asked.

They eventually left, but the aftermath was worse than all of the questioning. Our home was a shambles. More importantly, their intrusion pushed our marriage to the edge. I was shaken, but stubborn in my belief that something was not right.

The next day my supervisor summoned me to his office and told me I should be fired. He said the company did not employ drug dealers, but he was going to give me a break because I had been a loyal employee. If I was smart I would get back to work and forget it ever happened.

I was stunned. The possibility I could get fired over a leaf I brought back from the rainforest never once crossed my mind. I needed my job and planned to forget the whole thing. Then something happened that forever changed our lives.

A few weeks later, I was asked to report the latest results of our research to the Board of

Directors. The meeting did not go well. We were prepared to give our presentation, but were unexpectedly told it wasn't necessary because the program had been terminated. Some of us would be reassigned. Others would be laid off. That's all we were told before being abruptly dismissed from the meeting.

I felt ill and made a detour to the executive wash room. As I sat in a stall wondering how I would support my family, Wilbur Goth and his assistant, O.J. Renfield, entered the room.

"Did you see the news today?" asked Goth.

"Yes, it's escalating," said Renfield.

"War, crime, violence, famine, disease, earthquakes, tornadoes…the end is near," said Goth.

"Next they will turn on us," said Renfield.

"If the people discover how powerful they really are then there will be no controlling them," said Goth.

"We can't let that happen," said Renfield. "We must either kill them or weaken them with illness."

"Illness and fear of death make cowards of us all," said Goth.

"Now that we have the cure, we can unleash the virus," said Renfield.

"Has a test site been chosen yet?" asked Goth.

"Several small villages in the Middle East are

under consideration," said Renfield.

"Perfect," said Goth. "Just make certain it is blamed on terrorists."

"No problem," said Renfield. "The ground work has already been completed."

"Is there any progress on the development of a domestic delivery system?" asked Goth.

"Our new heartburn medication, Gutchriem, is showing great promise," answered Renfield.

"Does it effectively mask the virus?' asked Goth.

"The preliminary results are promising," answered Renfield.

"Good, I can't emphasize how important this is," said Goth. "We must have an effective means of spreading the virus to the general population that is totally fool proof," said Goth.

"Understood," said Renfield.

"Failure is not an option," said Goth.

"We will not fail," said Renfield.

"It is also critical that no one ever know we have a cure," said Goth.

"Who would have thought it," said Renfield. "A weed from the jungle wipes out viral infections."

"The damn thing is a wonder drug," said Goth. "It cures everything and restores optimal health. Hell, I bet we could live forever thanks to this little plant."

"It would wipe out the entire healthcare industry," said Renfield.

"It would destroy our business," said Mr. Goth. "We've made billions from the common cold alone."

"More importantly, we'd lose our ability to control the masses," said Renfield. "Besides, it could ruin all our plans."

"Once we eliminate the unsuitable masses, we will start all over and build our kind of society," said Goth.

"Only the chosen ones will be allowed to survive," said Renfield. "The rest will be fed to the worms."

"They must not get their hands on the cure," said Goth. "Have you had any luck finding and destroying the plants at their source?"

"No, the Amazonian Rainforest is huge," answered Renfield.

"If necessary, destroy the entire Rainforest," said Mr. Goth. "This plant grows like a weed and we want our farming operation to be the only source."

"It's already in the works," said Renfield. "We've ramped up our efforts to create a false market for rainforest products. We estimate two acres of rainforest are destroyed every second."

"Good," said Mr. Goth. "How long will it take to destroy the entire thing?"

"Thirty-five years at the current rate," said Renfield.

"Too damn long," said Goth. "How's Plan B going? Any leads from Bardough?"

"Nothing helpful," said Renfield. "All he remembers is meeting a native somewhere on the river bank. The Amazon River is four thousand miles long. That's too much riverbank to explore."

"Watch him carefully," said Mr. Goth. "Maybe he will lead us to the source. Once he does, then kill him."

CHAPTER 12

Holy crap! If this is true, then it explains why Gutchriem is making people sick. Goth is using it to deliver a bio-weapon that will murder millions of innocent people. This guy is a monster and I defended him in Court. To make matters worse, I convinced a jury Gutchriem is safe and then it put my mother in a coma. If it wasn't for me, Goth would be sitting in prison right now and Mom wouldn't be fighting for her life.

What have I done? My client is not only guilty, he is evil and should be behind bars.

My body was shaking so badly, I found it difficult to focus on my surroundings. When my eyes finally came to a rest, it was Ginny's face that I saw. Her eyes were calm, but I could see a fire smoldering just below the surface. She studied me closely.

"It has started," she said.

I nodded.

"Official corruption is wide spread," I said. "Discontent is growing. People are beginning to riot against unjust governments. It's only a matter of time before it explodes worldwide.

"The signs of decay that trigger Goth's plan to wipe us all out," she said.

"He's a psychopath," I said.

"Yes, he is," said Ginny.

"I kept him out of jail," I said.

"You couldn't have known," she said.

"No, I guess not," I said.

"The only relevant question is what are you going to do about it?" she said.

"We need to stop him," I said.

She nodded.

"How?" asked Ginny.

"We have to warn everybody," I said.

"Who would believe us?" she asked.

"You're right of course," I said. "We'll need clear and convincing evidence."

"How do we get it?" she asked.

I shrugged.

"Let's begin by talking to your dad," I said.

"So you believe he is my father?" she asked.

"It's weird how he looks like he should be your brother, but Weird has become the story of my life," I said. "Yes, I believe."

"Then there's hope," said Ginny.

I smiled and said, "Yes, there's hope."

Ginny looked thoughtful and said, "Until he returns there's something I want to ask you."

"Sure, ask anything you want," I said.

"Is there an us?" asked Ginny.

I think I may have stopped breathing, so I swallowed hard to kick start it again. When I could trust myself to speak, it came from the heart.

"All I've ever wanted is to be loved…ummm…errr…to be loved by you," I said.

"Yessss!" she said and threw her arms around me.

We held each other for a long time before reluctantly separating. Ginny looked thoughtful.

"Well there won't be much for us until we resolve your legal problems," she said. "Really, Grant, you're a lovable mess."

"Yeah, I've hit a rough spot," I admitted. "The criminal charges were taken care of by the military. They shut down the murder investigation in exchange for my silence about what really happened at the Center."

"What do you think really happened?" asked Ginny.

"I only know what I saw and that was a brief flash of images," I answered. "It's sort of like subliminal pictures that were burned into my mind."

"What did you see?" she asked.

"When the shooting started, people rushed the exits, but the doors remained closed," I said.

"Were they locked from the outside?" she asked.

"It sure looked that way to me," I answered.

"What else did you see?" she asked.

"They started shaking," I answered.

Ginny's hand flew to her mouth.

"Oh my god!" exclaimed Ginny. "I saw that too. At first, I thought it was an epileptic convulsion, before I realized that might happen to an individual, but not an auditorium full of people."

"That's true," I said.

"Is there something we could have done for them?" she asked.

"Maybe, but I was focused on getting us out of there and as far away from the shooter as possible," I answered.

She clutched herself and said, "I just remembered something. There was a hiss. I heard it between the shots."

"A hiss?" I asked.

She nodded.

"Like a cat?" I asked.

"No, it was more like gas escaping from a canister," she said.

"When I awoke after the shooting, the news

was on," I said. "They reported all of those people had been killed by an accidental gas leak."

"If it was a gas leak, they would have fallen asleep, wouldn't they?" she said.

I nodded.

"It seems highly unlikely it was a gas leak," I said. "Shaking is the first symptom of Gutchriem poisoning."

"All of those people couldn't have been suffering from acid reflux," she said.

"I agree, while chronic gut issues are at epidemic proportions, I doubt the entire audience was taking Gutchriem," I said.

"Do you think Goth has other ways to spread the virus?" asked Ginny.

"He's been working on it for years, so I would guess that he does," I said.

"Do you think the hiss was the sound of someone releasing the virus into the HVAC system?" she asked.

"It's possible," I answered.

"They planned to test their bio-weapon on a third world village, but I'm having a hard time imagining stone age people taking heartburn medicine," said Ginny.

"You're right," I said. "It makes sense that Goth has other delivery systems."

"Nothing about this lunatic makes much

sense," said Ginny.

I pointed to the journal.

"This entry is from twenty years ago," I said. "How does a madman fly under the radar for twenty years?"

"You can hide a lot of crazy with wealth," said Ginny. "Do you know if they ever actually used it on a village?"

I shook my head.

"If they disguised it well, then it could have blended in with hundreds of other terrorist attacks," I said.

"Dad might know," said Ginny.

"Yeah, he might," I agreed.

"We need to talk to him, but while we wait for his return, let's try to come up with some way to prove Goth is killing people," said Ginny.

"I may have a lead on that, but we'll need to get back to Louisville," I said.

"What is it?" she asked.

"I had a strange conversation with Zeke Kruthers after the trial," I said.

"I'm sorry, I don't know who that is," said Ginny.

"I sometimes forget you no longer live in Louisville," I said. "He's the prosecutor who believes Goth intentionally deceived the public about the risks of Gutchriem."

Ginny shook her head.

"You lawyers," she said. "One minute you're in Court fighting tooth and nail to beat each other into submission, and in the next, you're have drinks."

I shrugged my shoulders.

"It's a job that requires professionalism, Ginny," I said. "In most towns, the legal community is small. Without civility and professional courtesy, it would be a toxic community."

"I get that, but sometimes we hide behind concepts like professionalism to justify behavior that is inherently wrong," she said.

"There's a lot of truth to that," I said.

"So, tell me about this strange conversation with Mr. Kruthers after you soundly beat him in court and set Goth free," said Ginny.

I groaned, but the look in Ginny's eyes told me her comment was not intended to be critical.

"While we were waiting for the verdict, someone provided him with an envelope filled with documents," I said.

"What documents?" she asked.

"He wouldn't say," I answered.

"Who left them?" she asked.

"He thought I did," I said.

"I assume you didn't," she said.

I shook my head.

"What did he say about the documents?" she asked.

"He said they are a game changer," I answered.

"A game changer," she said.

I nodded.

"Pathogen is somehow involved," I said.

Ginny raised an eyebrow and said, "In what way?"

"He wouldn't say," I answered.

"Geez, what did he say?" she asked.

"He said my law firm is implicated," I said.

Ginny looked alarmed.

"Are you implicated?" she asked.

"I don't see how," I said. "It has something to do with my boss, John Biggs."

"Are you talking about the co-worker who hung himself?" she asked.

I nodded.

"He killed himself after he spoke to Zeke Kruthers about the documents," I said.

"We need to know what those documents say," she said.

"I agree, but ethical considerations may prevent Zeke from telling us," I said.

"Then we need to find another way," she said.

"It would help if we knew who provided them

to Zeke," I said.

"Any ideas?" she asked.

I shook my head.

"Someone who wants to take Pathogen down," I answered.

"That could be a long list," she said.

"Yep," I said. "There's more."

"What else did he say?" she asked.

"He told me to look into my father's death," I said.

"I thought it was an accident," she said.

"Yeah, me too, but now I'm not so sure," I said.

"Do you think his death has something to do with the documents?" she said.

"It's hard to say for sure, but it was the only clue he would give me," I said.

"Did he say anything else?" she asked.

"One more thing," I answered. "He said he was afraid of these people and warned me to watch my back."

"A Federal prosecutor said that?" she asked.

I nodded.

"Who's he afraid of…and why?" she murmured.

"There's something I haven't told you yet," I said.

"I'm not going to like this, am I?" she asked.

"Probably not," I said.

"Tell me," she said.

"Do you remember me telling you about the little man I bumped into outside of John's office just before I discovered his body?," I asked.

"Yes, you called him Mr. Bowtie or something else equally colorful," she said.

"Mr. Suit," I said.

"Mr. Suit," she repeated.

"It was expensive," I said.

"The suit," she said.

I nodded.

"Mr. Suit showed up at the hospital and threatened me," I said.

"What kind of threats?" she asked.

"He threatened to torture me," I answered.

Ginny inhaled sharply.

"Torture!" she said.

"They had me strapped to a bed and Sadistic Doctor was planning to run electricity through my brain," I said.

"Electroshock…I thought they stopped that years ago," she said.

I shrugged.

"Evidently not," I said.

She shuddered.

"It seems so barbaric," she said.

"I think of it as the little death, because it's just

one twist of the knob below the electric chair," I said.

"Don't they at least use anesthesia?" she said.

"Sadistic Doctor never used it on me," I said.

Ginny looked appalled.

"That's…that's…torture!" she said.

"I can handle it," I said.

"Because you've been through this before," she said.

"Yes, I have," I said.

"When we were kids…after the incident with mother," she said.

I nodded.

Her eyes filled with tears.

"I'm so sorry, Grant," she said.

"Ginny, you have nothing to be sorry for," I said.

She hung her head and sobbed.

I put the journal down and went to her. She laid her head on my chest and all the years of heartache came pouring out…from both of us.

When the sobs subsided, I wiped the last of her tears with my thumb and said, "There's more."

She sighed.

"Of course there is," she said. "What else?"

"Mr. Suit thought I had something that belonged to him," I said.

"What?" she asked.

"Confidential files," I answered.

"What files?" she asked.

I shrugged.

"Do you think he's looking for the prosecutor's envelope of documents?" she asked.

"It could be anything, but that seems highly probable," I said.

"We need to talk to him," she said.

"Yes, we do," I said.

"There's one more thing," I said.

She raised any eyebrow.

"Mr. Suit was looking for your father," I said.

"Oh my God, so was Slotter," she said. "Do you think they are working for Goth?"

"Everything is pointing in that direction," I said.

"We need to talk to Dad," she said.

I nodded.

"We should talk to him when he returns," I said. "In the meantime, I'd like to finish reading his journal."

"I'll let you finish reading while I do some thinking," she said.

She tried to smile, but it was grim.

Once again, I saw the grit she used to build a multi-billion dollar company within ten years of graduating from college. I no longer carried this burden alone. Together we could succeed. With that comforting thought, I returned to her father's journal.

* * *

I had to do something to stop them. If I confronted them or went to the police, they would just deny it. Besides, the incident with the Feds reminded me that they owned the police. I hoped someone out there would listen.

Unfortunately, I had no proof. I needed to get more of the plant. It was risky. They had terrorized my family and threatened to arrest me. On the other hand, life had handed me an important task. I knew I couldn't walk away from it. My conscience wouldn't permit it.

I thought about it for days before deciding it was time to return to the rainforest and find the source of Great Mother. I figured once I had the medicine in hand, then I could figure out how to deliver it to the people. Free of illness, they will enjoy optimal health for the first time in their lives. This will end the healthcare crisis and destroy Pathogen before it destroys us. I just needed a way to slip away without their watchdogs following me.

The first wave of layoffs hit our department,

but they kept me on. I needed the money, but I hated working for these people. If I quit, then I might tip them off that I was on to them. I decided to use an upcoming conference in Vegas as cover to look for the plant.

In order to keep you safe, I decided to keep the details of the plan to myself. Besides, the Feds scared your mother and she wanted me to drop the whole thing. It led to terrible arguments whenever I tried to discuss returning to the rainforest. I didn't want to leave you, but I saw no other way. To keep you safe, I asked Robert Li to look after the two of you if anything ever happened to me.

* * *

My father!

I looked up and saw Ginny studying me. There was a strange look to her face that reminded me of a mother looking after her young. I wasn't sure what it meant, but it made me feel safe.

It was a new feeling for me and that seemed wrong somehow. How can a grown man not be intimately familiar with safety? Such a man would have spent his life in a fight or flight mode…and I am such a man.

"Your father asked my dad to watch over you," I said.

"Yes, he did," said Ginny.

"Then Dad let us both down," I said.

She shook her head.

"He did not let me down," she said.

"My dad let me down," I said.

"No, Grant," said Ginny. "Think this through."

"What do you mean?" I asked.

"They tried to kill my dad," she said.

I nodded.

Ginny waited.

"When did your father die?" she asked.

I did some quick mental math. Dad was killed by a hit-and-run driver around the same time Ginny's father left for South America. Then it hit me.

"Do you think the hit-and-run was intentional?" I asked.

Ginny didn't answer, but I detected a slight nod and asked, "Do you think they killed my dad?"

"I don't know Grant, but these people seem capable of anything," said Ginny.

They kidnapped Ginny, shot us both, tortured me, and tried to kill her father. To force a motorcycle off the road and leave a small boy's parents to die in a ditch requires a certain level of cold-heartedness that only the worst of villains have. Yes, they are capable of anything.

"Could this be what Zeke Kruthers was talking about when he suggested I investigate Dad's death?" I asked.

"It seems likely to me he was trying to point you in the direction of your own client, Wilbur Goth, and his pharmaceutical company, Pathogen," she said.

"If he's right, then Goth stole my childhood by killing Dad and turning Mom into a bed ridden paraplegic for the last twenty years," I said.

"We have to do something about Goth," said Ginny.

I nodded absent mindedly, but I was really thinking about Mom in a coma and fighting for her life once again, thanks to Goth. More anger than I ever thought I had began to rise to the surface. Knowing there is nothing noble about anger, I tried to push it down, but it was irrepressible.

To Ginny's credit she didn't interfere. Instead she sat quietly and bore witness to the pain I had buried so deep I was no longer aware it existed. It was Great Mother that pulled me out of that hell and back into the world of the living.

"Do you think Great Mother could help Mom?" I asked.

"Yes…yes, I do," answered Ginny.

Her quiet confidence in this strange jungle plant calmed me. I exhaled slowly and decided to find a way to give it to Mom as soon as we returned to Kentucky. In the meantime, I wanted to finish her father's journal, so I continued reading where I had left off.

* * *

I changed my flight and flew into Ecuador. As soon as I arrived in Quito, I rented a jeep and drove to Manaus. It was a brutal, five day, three thousand mile journey, but I wanted to make absolutely certain they couldn't follow me. I practically lived on Yerba Mate that I drank through a silver straw.

In Manaus I chartered a small plane to tour the Amazon rainforest. I hoped by some miracle I could find the shaman who healed me. He gave me Great Mother once. Maybe he would do it again.

It was an insane plan. The rainforest is huge and it all looked the same from the air. The flight was unproductive and I was discouraged as we turned back. The only other idea I had was to recreate the river cruise we did on our honeymoon. That would take much longer and my memories of the river were not good.

I took one last look at the jungle below and wondered if I would ever find the plant. As I peered out the window, I saw a military helicopter approaching our plane. Curious, I studied it closely. As it got closer I could see there were gunmen at the open door with weapons pointed in our direction. I was about to tell the pilot about the helicopter when a rocket was fired in our direction.

CHAPTER 13

Her father's story was interrupted when a young woman entered. Like all of the Guardians, she looked to be twenty-something, but had the presence of someone much older. Most people seem to become more tolerant as they age. Being at ease with the world around them, gives them an air of dignity that can't be faked. The young woman was clearly very comfortable in her own skin.

Like the others, she was nude. As far as I could tell, there wasn't a scar or blemish anywhere on her body. She was flawless. I'm embarrassed to say that I thought the Guardians all looked alike when I first arrived, but the longer I stayed with them the easier it was to tell them apart.

It was the little differences that set them apart from each other. For instance, this woman wore her black silky hair in a long braid that she pulled over a swimmer's shoulder and let fall gently around the curve of her right breast. Just below her nipple, the braid split into three braids for about four inches and then came back together into one before finishing its descent in a curly flourish.

Smiling she said, "I'm called Coral. I was sent to fetch you to your bath."

Ginny raised an eyebrow.

"They think we stink," I said with a grin.

"Like a skunk," quipped Ginny.

Coral led us down the path leading to the bubbling springs. Along the way, we passed two women playfully fondling each other. Coral paid the giggling couple no attention. I cut my eyes to Ginny. She cast them a curious look, but said nothing about it.

Much of the community was gathered near the fountain. It is a natural formation of rock vaguely shaped like a couple entwined in an erotic embrace. Water emerged from a hot spring deep within the Earth and flowed between the couple's legs before emptying into the steaming pool.

Eric was surrounded by a group of beautiful women about twenty yards to the left of the Fountain. Camo Girl was nowhere in sight. Layah was swimming laps in the cooler water nearby. Ginny tested the hot springs with her big toe.

Nodding her approval, she said to no one in particular, "Oh, I so need this."

She was a little too eager and lost her footing on the steps leading into the pool. It was a good thing I was following her because she fell right into my arms. Startled, she looked back and caught a glimpse of the bliss radiating from me. With a sigh, she slowly relaxed into me and stayed there a little longer than necessary.

It felt good, maybe a little too good. I was getting very turned on again. I willed it down. It refused to comply. I couldn't hide behind Ginny forever. Shit. I was screwed.

This was a growing problem that seemed to be happening when other people were watching. I never thought of myself as an exhibitionist. In fact, you might say I've been obsessed with avoiding public displays at all costs. This visible state of arousal was yet another example of the many ways my life had turned upside down over the last few days.

I figured Ginny felt my erection because her head suddenly whipped around. Her attention didn't help. I burned with a mix of embarrassment and desire. It didn't take her long to figure out my predicament and her mouth formed a mischievous smile that I'm not sure I liked. This one was going to cost me big time.

She laughed. The tension broke. The beast retreated in the face of laughter, but not completely.

The intimate moment was interrupted by a shout from Eric.

"Mr. Johnson…oh Mr. Johnson, would the four of you like to join us?" shouted Eric.

When I raised an eyebrow, Eric cut his eyes to my predicament. It's possible I may have ground my molars together in exasperation. Eric could be so sophomoric at times. Addressing my body parts as Mr. Johnson was the kind of juvenile behavior he thrived upon.

I was about to decline Mr. Subtlety's invitation, but both Ginny and Coral headed in his direction. Eric does that to women. He draws them in with some kind of powerful magnetic force of personality that has always mystified me. I let out a sigh and followed the girls.

"Where's Camo Girl?" I asked.

With a twinkle in his eye Eric said, "I think I wore the poor girl out. She's napping. By the way, her name is Anna, but I think I prefer Camo Girl. You've got to love that outrageous getup she had on. Not that it exists anymore. They burned our clothes, you know. Now that's a level of commitment to naturism I can respect."

Coral eyed Eric like he was a special treat.

"Your clothes aren't necessary," she said. "It's warm here and we have nothing to hide from each other."

Ginny chimed in.

"Besides, clothing collects odors and I'm fresh out of deodorant," she said.

"I love your natural scent," I mumbled under my breath, but Ginny heard me.

"You could have mentioned that before I sunk all the way to my chin in this delicious hot bath," said Ginny.

"I could have, but clean is good too," I said. "You're yummy with or without cooties."

Ginny's eyes widened slightly and her breath caught in her chest for just a split second, but I saw it. She started to say something, but then stopped. Finally, whatever she intended to say was replaced with a smile that began in her eyes before spreading to her lips.

"What are cooties?" asked Coral.

That started a round of laughter that brought tears to my eyes. When the laughter finally subsided, Eric leaned over and whispered something in Coral's ear.

In one smooth movement, her hand slipped into the clear water, and for the first time, I watched another man grow from his humble state of rest into an angry beast. I had no idea Eric was so well-endowed.

Coral slipped under the water and took him

into her mouth. Eric grunted just before his eyes rolled back into his head. The girl must have been half fish. She was down there a long time by my reckoning. It was way longer than any normal person could have held their breath.

I'm not sure how my hand found its way between Ginny's legs, but it was there exploring the soft petals of her flesh. As if she sensed the tentativeness of my touch, she let out a soft moan and pressed herself more firmly against my hand.

Encouraged by her reaction, I slipped the tip of my forefinger just inside of her. Her moan got a little deeper. It stirred an equally deep place inside of me and I suddenly had to have her, right then. I pulled her onto my lap and plunged into her.

I wanted to get as deep as I possibly could and held nothing back. She took it. She took all of it without a whimper, without any resistance. That was a first for me. It was as if we were made to fit. This time it was my lips that allowed a moan to escape.

It was a good thing she was on top. Otherwise, I would not have lasted much longer than the initial plunge. While I had pulled her onto my lap, Ginny was now in charge and her eyes held me in a deep embrace.

Without moving, we looked deeply into each other. It was then that I really saw her for the first time. I really saw her and in that instant I ceased to exist. There was only us.

The rest of our bath time was soothing and relaxing as we basked in the after-glow of love making. I was beginning to like this communal bath a lot.

Afterwards, Ginny went for food and I returned to the journal. Gratefully, she promised to bring me something to eat. Grinning, she told me I needed to keep my strength up. I like the way her grin takes up all of her face like Wonderland's Cheshire cat. With that she sashayed off in the direction of the cooking fire.

I picked up her father's journal and continued where I left off.

* * *

Our plane was hit by the rocket. I'm pretty sure we crashed, but the only thing I can say for sure is I lost consciousness.

The last thing I remember as we tore through the tree tops was the pilot repeatedly saying, "You fired on me! You weren't supposed to fire on me."

When I came to, there was a beautiful woman

leaning over me. Her hand gently caressed my cheek. Her big brown eyes sparkled with an amazing light. I had never seen anything like her and was certain she was an angel.

She spoke, but her words didn't make any sense. The only word I recognized was "Namaste," which means the creator in me honors the creator in you. So, it's possible she was speaking Sanskrit. Which was very weird considering we were in South America.

The Angel gave her head a little shake and switched to Spanish. When that didn't work, she tried several more languages in rapid succession before she settled on English.

"My name is Layah," she said. "How do you feel?"

I wiggled my toes, clinched my left hand into a tight fist, and then rolled my head from side to side. Satisfied they seemed to be in good working order, I did a full body scan. Everything seemed to be in tip top shape. In fact, I felt great. I hadn't felt that good since the shaman healed me on my honeymoon.

"I feel amazing, but that makes no sense," I answered. "Half of the airplane's wing was shot off and we went down fast. I should be dead right now."

"We saw Quetzalcoatl blasted from the sky by

a helicopter and went to investigate," she said. "The crash left a path of destruction in the forest. Countless plants were wounded and more than a few were completely destroyed. We saved as many of our four legged brothers and sisters as we could."

Layah folded her hands and placed them over her heart. With bowed head she said a prayer of thanks for their sacrifice and then opened her arms wide above her head, releasing their spirit to the creator. As if on cue, a beam of sunlight cut through the dense foliage and illuminated her face. It only lasted a few breaths before the light softened and she continued her story.

"The crash site was scattered with torn and twisted metal", she said. "Foul smelling smoke rose from burning chunks of plastic plane parts. No one moved to stop the fires. Instead, we left them to cleanse this sacred place."

"You were found lying in a crumpled heap at the base of an ancient Yerba Mate tree where you had been thrown by chance upon impact. We pulled you from death just before the soldiers came. After searching the area, they once again mounted the vimana and flew away."

"Vimana?" I asked.

With a little shake of the head, she said, "I think you call them helicopters."

"Isn't vimana the name for an ancient Indian flying machine?' I asked.

"It's not quite as ancient as you might think, but yes," she said.

I had no idea why she would say they are not ancient, since the vimana were discussed in fifth century B.C. Hindu texts. That seemed pretty old to me, but I had no desire to argue with the angel and decided to change the subject.

"You saved me," I said. "Thank you."

"Yes, but you have persistent enemies," said Layah. "The soldiers came back many times, but the jungle was not friendly to them and they eventually abandoned their search."

I needed to know who was behind this and asked, "Did the pilot survive? I have a few questions I want to ask him."

She shook her head.

"No, he was beyond help," said Layah.

"His injuries must have been serious," I said.

"It's less about the extent of injury and more about timing," she said. "We can heal any harm if we catch it in time."

I decided to take a chance and asked, "With Great Mother?"

Layah nodded and said, "Get some rest. We'll talk more later."

She brushed the hair out of my eyes and

chanted a strange lullaby, "He rides on the wings of a morning star. Oh, great serpent, uncover all that lies hidden below."

It felt as if electricity pulsed from her. I wanted to touch more than her finger tips, but I was a married man. A wife and child awaited my return. It was time to turn away from my unfaithful thoughts.

As I drifted off to sleep I wondered about the weird turn of events that delivered me to the exact place I needed to be. I had found the mother of all medicinal herbs!

CHAPTER 14

Ginny arrived with food and insisted I eat something. I'm not sure, but I think it was Anaconda Stew. Sometimes it's best to avoid asking too many questions.

"Do you want to talk about it?" asked Ginny.

I wasn't sure what she meant by "It," but I knew enough about women to know she wanted to talk about "It". I decided the safest course was to keep my answer simple, but broad.

"Yes, I do," I answered.

She waited patiently for more. I didn't know what to say, so I said nothing in the hopes she would speak up and tell me what was on her mind. That didn't work very well. Ginny proved to be more patient than me.

Given the onslaught of her frustratingly patient gaze, I ventured a guess she wanted to talk about our lovemaking at the Fountain. Maybe she wanted me to reassure her…to tell her that we have a future together and that I love her.

These were the thoughts that led me to say, "I don't want you to worry about what happened in the water earlier."

Ginny went completely still. I couldn't even detect the gentle rise and fall of her breath. She looked at me with cold deadpan eyes. I have to admit, it was more than a little scary seeing her like this. When she finally spoke, her voice was hard.

"That was just a fuck, Grant," she said. "Don't get your panties in a bunch."

She could have jumped up and down on my chest with six inch stilettos and it wouldn't have hurt as badly as those two sentences spoken with such coldness. I didn't know what to say. What happened in the water was more than that for me…way more.

On the other hand, a part of me was not surprised by her attitude. It is certainly a view held by my wife. I guess I had come to expect it from all women.

Me…well I wanted something more. I wanted the fairy tale. I wanted happily ever after. I wanted to be reunited with my soul mate…my twin flame. Plato once wrote that love is nothing more than the desire to be whole again. That's what I wanted…to be whole. When we made love, I was whole for the first time in my life.

Ginny is my other half, but I didn't have the skill-set to handle her rejection, so I turned away.

I must confess it took a while for my vision to clear enough to resume reading her father's journal.

* * *

Happy Birthday Ginny! You are ten today and I hope your day is filled with much joy and happiness. I imagine you are growing like a weed. I wish I was there to see it. I miss you more than ever.

It hasn't been easy for me to stay away. At first I was eager to return. I missed you and I was determined to put a stop to Pathogen's evil plans. Great Mother can cure the virus, but I also discovered it does much more. It restores the body to a state of optimal health. Free of the fear of illness and functioning at full capacity, people can focus on making a better life for themselves. It is a game changer and I wanted to share Great Mother with the world.

The Guardians convinced me it is not yet time. They told me that someone else was destined to bring Great Mother to the world, but I still have a role to play. Instead, they invited me to stay with them and assist in their cause. I was reluctant to abandon you and your mother. On the other hand, I knew Pathogen would kill me if

I returned. It was also possible that they would harm you to get to me and that was not acceptable.

The Guardians promised they would protect you. I found it hard to imagine. They are a gentle and kind-hearted group of people who still live in the stone ages. Besides, you are my responsibility, not theirs. For days, I struggled to find a solution. The days turned into weeks and then months. Time made the decision for me.

As the months flew by, more than my body was healed. Living with these people has calmed my mind and restored my spirit. Men and women live as equals. There is no conflict between the sexes. The men do not control the village's resources. Women do not trade their bodies for security. Pleasure is shared by all. No one is exploited.

In this garden, they live as I imagine Adam and Eve lived in the Garden of Eden. They have no concept of property. If someone is hungry, then they are fed. They wear no clothes, so there are no expensive shopping sprees. No one lives in a mansion or slum. They sleep together in a shared building. There is no competition between them and no rules of the game. They do not fear each other, so there is no need for government and law. They are truly free.

There is something else you should know. There was a birth of a beautiful boy. Layah's delivery was quick and painless. The entire village witnessed his grand entry into the world. He was passed from person to person.

Each one said the same thing, "Welcome, my son."

When he was passed to me, I looked into his beautiful blue eyes and wondered how that happened in a village full of brown eyes. Then it hit me, I alone have blue eyes. Ginny darling, you have a brother.

As I read her father's journal, Ginny was as quiet as a church mouse. I tried to pretend she wasn't in the room, but failed miserably. I was fully aware of her presence, each and every minute. I felt her with all of my being. Still, it startled me when she spoke.

"I'm sorry," she said.

I wanted to tell her it was nothing, but that wasn't true and it caught in my throat. It was something to me. What happened at the Fountain was extremely important to me. The way she devalued it was painful and I had to choke back tears.

It wasn't like me to be so emotional. I was turning into someone I didn't recognize, someone I didn't know very well. Yet, somehow it felt real. I felt more authentic than I ever remember being, so I followed Ch'ing's advice and embraced the emotions churning inside of me.

When I finally pulled myself together, I managed to say in a croaking sort of way, "It was more than a fuck for me."

Ginny stared at me with the most profound amazement on her face. She looked at me like I couldn't possibly be real. Like I was a sweet dream and she would wake up any second only to find herself alone once again.

It was her turn to choke on words I never heard. It was her turn to struggle with strange new emotions. I could see the emotional symphony play out on her face and in her body language. It was complex. It was rich. It was deep. When she finally pulled herself together, her voice was soft.

"When I returned with the food, I intended to discuss dad's journal," said Ginny. "I never thought we would be having this discussion. You caught me by surprise and I guess I misread your intent. I'm sorry I upset you."

I scrambled to make sense of it. We had this beautiful experience and then everything turned upside down in the blink of an eye. We made a deep soul-confirming connection, but then abruptly disconnected when she misread my intent. I wanted to understand so we would never repeat it, but came up with nothing. It was damn frustrating.

I was completely in the dark, but then a light bulb went off. This was about all those years when she needed me the most and I wasn't there for her. She must have thought I was once again distancing myself from her. Ginny, was trying to protect herself. It was time to set the record straight.

"Ginny, I'm the one who should be apologizing," I said. "I fell in love with you when I was five years old. Not once have I stopped loving you. I'm ashamed I let your mother scare me away. If you will have me, I promise to stand by you no matter what life throws at us."

Ginny's eyebrows shot up so high it gave her wide eyes an exaggerated comical appearance. It's possible I caught her by surprise.

"Did you...did you just propose?" asked Ginny.

I swallowed hard. It all hung in the balance and there was nothing for me to do, but to speak the simple truth.

"Yes, I believe I did," I answered.

As an afterthought I added, "I think I should ask for your father's permission, don't you?"

In answer to my question, Ginny flew into my arms, but it caught me by surprise and we tumbled to the ground, where she proceeded to smother me with kisses. I didn't mind one bit.

That's exactly where Eric found us. Being Eric and all he couldn't help but joke about finding me flat on my back with Ginny in total control.

"I can't leave you kids alone for five minutes without finding the two of you rolling around in the dirt," said Eric. "What's up with that?"

Ginny broke for air and said, "We're celebrating."

"Celebrating what…the loss of Grant's virginity?" quipped Eric.

"She said yes!" I said.

"Yes…you mean the big yes…the all in capitals YES?" asked Eric.

I nodded vigorously.

"You proposed marriage to this beautiful woman?" asked Eric.

I nodded even more vigorously.

"And…and she said yes," sputtered Eric.

"Yep, can you believe it!" I exclaimed.

Eric gave each of us a hand and pulled us to our feet.

"Well it's about fucking time," said Eric. "Come here you two and give me a hug."

"Ooooh, time for what?" asked Camo Girl. "A little foursome, maybe?"

I froze. She had somehow slipped in on us. There was no way in hell I was into that. I did not want to share Ginny with anyone.

The people who know me the best came to my rescue. Both Ginny and Eric shook their heads, but it was Ginny who spoke first.

"Not with my husband, you don't," said Ginny.

Eric chimed in, "Oh, that would be like incest or something. Grant and I are brothers. There are plenty of other playmates around here."

"Husband?" asked Camo Girl.

Ginny's grin was even bigger than the wide Cheshire Cat grin she usually flashes. Her head nods were equally exaggerated.

Camo Girl rushed to Ginny and threw her arms around her. There might have been a shrill attempt at speech that accompanied the hug. Who can say what language that is, except most women seem to speak it fluently.

Eric threw his arm over my shoulders and pulled me in tight as he said in a husky tone, "Way to go, Grant."

There might have been tears in his eyes as well. Mine too, for that matter. Hell, we were all crying up a storm when Pony Tail showed up.

"What's all the fuss about?" asked Pony Tail.

These people lived very casual lives. I wasn't sure whether they would share our joy over the engagement. I shouldn't care, but they had gotten under my skin very quickly. Despite the rough start with Pony Tail, he was Ginny's brother and I wanted his blessing. It was odd, but I realized I wanted all of their blessings.

"There's going to be a wedding," said Eric.

"I love…love weddings," said Camo Girl.

"Really?" asked Eric. "You sure don't seem like the marrying type to me."

Camo Girl dropped her chin slightly and punched Eric in the arm with a hard right hand. As far as punches go, it was pretty damn respectable. Eric loves a good fight and I think her martial skill surprised him too.

"I'll have you know, mister, that I've been successfully married four times," said Camo Girl.

"Is that all?" asked Eric as he rubbed his arm. "Why at your age, you should have at least six under your belt by now."

With narrowed eyes Camo Girl said, "Funny guy…I'm only twenty four."

Eric gave his arm a little shake and said, "I can't speak to how good you are at marriage, but I can confirm you pack a respectable wallop in that right hand of yours."

"Pussy," said Camo Girl, but there was no real contempt in her voice. In fact, she was beaming with pride.

Four failed marriages by twenty four. Geez! Right on the tail of my judgmental thoughts it hit me. I'm already married. I have a wife.

"Ginny, you are glowing," said Pony Tail. "It must be your wedding we're talking about and I can tell by the look of terror on Grant's face he's the groom. We better have the wedding quickly before he loses his nerve."

Ginny's glow quickly dimmed as she cut her eyes to me. This was something that could go South very quickly if I didn't nip it in the bud. The divorce was only a formality and it shouldn't take too long to wrap up once I got back to Louisville.

"There is nothing I want more than to marry Ginny," I said.

I heard a voice behind me say, "Good. Then it's settled. We'll have the wedding tomorrow."

Lao Tzu once wrote that the Great Tao lowers the high and raises the low. I had just tumbled from the peak of happiness into the depths of despair. Okay, maybe that's a tad bit melodramatic. The fact is, I wanted to marry Ginny tomorrow, but having two wives is against the law.

On the other hand, Ginny was riding high. She rushed toward me with arms outstretched and face aglow with happiness. I raised mine to accept her embrace, but she swept right past them and threw her arms around a curvaceous Hispanic woman of undetermined age.

Unlike these gentle giants who call themselves the Guardians, this woman was maybe 5'4". Although she was the shortest person in the room, there was something about her that made her larger than life. I think maybe it was her eyes. They were filled with an ocean of wisdom.

"Marguerite," shouted Ginny. "I can't believe you're here!"

Ginny had told me about Marguerite. Once upon a time, Marguerite was Ginny's nanny, but I think she was much more to Ginny than just a babysitter. She was Ginny's lifeline. With an absent father and a bat shit crazy mother, she was more relevant than her own family. You might say Marguerite was all the support she had.

Ginny told me she had planned a reunion during her trip to Louisville, but Marguerite never showed up. Oddly, that was about the same time that my martial arts teacher, Ch'ing, disappeared. Of all the damn places for her to materialize, this remote village in the middle of the rainforest was the last I'd have guessed.

Ginny laid her head on Marguerite's shoulder and wept. I could be mistaken, but it sounded to me like Marguerite was purring as she stroked her hair. When Ginny's sobs passed, Marguerite kissed the top of her head and turned to me.

"Well, you've grown into a handsome young man," said Marguerite.

Even though she was looking at me, I figured she was talking to Pony Tail, since I had never met this woman in my life. It was difficult, but I managed to break her hypnotic gaze and cut my eyes to Pony Tail thinking he'd reply to her compliment. When he didn't, I returned my attention to her.

"Yes, Grant, I'm speaking to you," said Marguerite.

"Have we met?" I asked.

"I've been watching over you from the beginning," she answered.

"You mean, like a guardian angel or something?" I asked.

Of course, my question was intended as a joke. I followed it with a laugh so weak, it embarrassed even me. She smiled anyway and it warmed the dark corners of my being. It felt like her smile came from the heart of the Earth, as if she was born of its very core.

"Something like that," was her simple

response, but that smile said so much more.

I believed her. It felt good knowing someone had been watching over me. At times it seemed like I was drifting through the days of my life without any real direction. At other times, I felt like I was getting more than my fair share of troubles. Marguerite made me feel like my life was on course after all.

"I've done the best I could under the circumstances," I said.

"It's okay, Grant," she said. "There is no need to make excuses before you've made your confession."

I couldn't imagine what she wanted me to confess. After all, I was raised Catholic and had spent my fair share of time in the confessional making up sins to confess to our parish priest. I didn't trust him with the truth and always wanted to get away from him as fast as I could.

Later, when he abruptly left the parish, no one would say why, but I overhead an adult whispering something about little Timmy Spreeng and the terrible things that awful priest made him do.

I wasn't sure what that meant, but one day he asked me to undress completely before I put on my altar boy robes. I didn't do it, because the Fat Lady said I'd be punished if I ever undressed in front of anyone again.

Afterwards, Father Pediman took me off the altar boy schedule. That was okay with me. I didn't really like how much time I was spending in church anyway. I'd much rather be in the woods and was glad to be free of his altar.

I needed to tell these people that my divorce was not yet final, but timing is everything and this reconciliation with Ginny felt fragile. Circumstances beyond my control were forcing me to deal with the unexpected consequences of my failed marriage before I was ready and I didn't like it.

I sighed. A relationship must be built on truth or it will never last. It was time to stop whining and tell these people the truth.

"I'm still married," I said.

Marguerite studied me closely and asked a question I didn't expect.

"What do you think marriage is?" asked Marguerite.

The lawyer in me spoke up and said, "It's a legal binding agreement to share one's life and worldly goods with another person."

Marguerite raised an eyebrow, but said nothing. Instead she waited for more. I felt like there was something better inside of me to give. It was something more real than the legal bullshit

I had just spouted. I swallowed. Marguerite wanted more than legalese and Ginny was looking crushed by my comments.

"It's completion," I said. "Like closing a circle. Ginny completes me."

Marguerite nodded her approval.

"Dude," said Eric softly.

Camo Girl dabbed at a tear in the corner of her eye.

Pony Tail gripped my shoulder and said softly, "Yes."

Ginny closed the gap between us in two quick steps. At first I thought she was going to throw her arms around me, but she stopped just short and held me with her eyes.

I liked what I saw in Ginny's eyes and would have been content to gaze into them, but slowly she stretched a hand to my cheek and caressed it ever so lightly with the back of her finger tips. A spark of electricity crackled between us and some of the tension I had been carrying around for the last few days melted away.

Ginny's breath quickened. In anticipation of her touch, my breathing matched pace with hers. I wasn't disappointed. She curled her hand behind my neck and then pulled me into a kiss. I had never experienced anything like it. The kiss filled an ocean of loneliness with love and I knew that I would never be the same.

The sky exploded and the Earth shook. I was thinking that was some damn kiss, when Layah rushed in and pointed a finger at Camo Girl.

"The enemy is here," said Layah.

Camo Girl's eyes darted wildly about, as if she was looking for an escape route. Having found none, she puffed herself up and started to say something, when a bullet knocked her to her knees. At first she seemed confused, but then a wave of acceptance washed over her face.

Her last words were, "Victor…forgive me."

The next round of gunfire missed the mark, but we got the message. It was time to fight or flee. It was Marguerite who took charge.

"They're here," she shouted. "We need to move, now!"

CHAPTER 15

My grandmother's chickens liked to hide their eggs from time to time. As hard as she tried, she couldn't find them all and a few were left to rot in their hiding places. I once stepped on one of the bad ones and will never forget the awful smell. It took days to get rid of it. Spent gunpowder has a distinctive odor, but it smells faintly of rotten eggs.

I scanned our surroundings for signs of the enemy, but blue smoke obscured my vision. I could see enough to tell we were surrounded. The forest had become a dangerous place once again.

"There's not much time," said Marguerite. "We must move quickly."

"Who are they?" asked Eric.

"Lost souls," answered Marguerite. She pointed to a cache of weapons and added, "Grab whatever you need and follow me."

Ginny chose a blade the size of a steak knife. Eric grabbed a short spear and I had an axe. Pony Tail carried a bow and quiver of arrows.

Marguerite waived off a blow gun saying she had her own defenses.

We used the heaviest smoke as cover to slip quietly past the soldiers. Marguerite led us deeper into the forest. Thinking we had made it out safely, I began to relax when she suddenly stopped and motioned us down. Ginny was following a little too closely and bumped into my back.

"Sorry," she whispered as she stepped on my foot.

The misstep cost her balance. When she tried to recover she cut me with her knife. I let out a yelp and whipped around to take the offending blade from her when I felt the sting of a bullet whizzing past my ear. I had a vision of an earless Vincent van Gogh and fought back a wave of panic.

I released the pressure on the cut and was using the bloody hand to make sure my ear was intact, when the bushes parted and a man carrying a machete two handed above his head leapt toward Ginny's back. I pushed her aside and exploded into him.

The next thing I remember were voices asking me if I was all right. I opened my eyes. I felt a hand on my bicep jiggling my arm. The voice sounded like it was coming from a tunnel.

"Grant, what happened to you?" asked Ginny.

The faces hovering above me gradually came into focus. I was flat on my back. Something was pressing into my kidneys. I smelled blood and wondered if it was mine.

"Grant?"

It was Ginny again.

There was a sharp pain in my chest. My knees felt weak. I opened my eyes.

"Where are we?" I asked.

Marguerite asked, "Do you remember what happened?"

I didn't have a clue and said, "I remember Ginny was attacked by a man with a snake tattoo. After that…nothing."

"Snake tattoo…was it wrapped around his right arm?" asked Ginny.

"Yes," I answered. "I've seen it before. The first time was one of the women who grabbed me in Manaus."

"So have I, Grant," said Ginny. "Match Breath had a tattoo like that."

We turned to Marguerite and Pony Tail for an explanation. It was Pony Tail who answered.

"Slavers," said Pony Tail.

Marguerite looked troubled and said, "That particular serpent tattoo is the brand for a secret society of slave traders who call themselves

Knights of the Golden Circle."

"So Wife Beater and her group of freaks were slave traders," I said.

Pony Tail nodded.

"They are well-trained and relentless," said Pony Tail. "Once they begin a job, they never give up until their mission is accomplished. If one of them goes down, two take his place."

"What could slavers possibly want with us?" I asked.

"Match Breath planned to sell me to a brothel," said Ginny. "Maybe they had a brothel in mind for you."

"Very funny, my beautiful fiancée," I said, "but Meat Cleaver wanted to split your pretty head open, not turn you into a sex slave."

Ginny's face lit up, "You think my head is pretty?"

In answer to her question, I took her in my arms and kissed the top of her head.

Eric pointed to a pile of bodies and said, "Dude, I've never seen you fight like that. You went berserk. Coiling and striking with incredible speed. After you dispatched Meat Cleaver, you killed four more in less than a minute. What the hell got into you?"

I shrugged, "I wasn't about to let those men harm Ginny."

Eric stuck his lower lip out in an exaggerated pout, "That was pretty damn selfish, you know. You could have left one or two for me."

Eric loves a good fight and I wasn't surprised by his comment, but the rest of the group looked at me like there was something else bothering them. I had no idea what it might be, so I waited for one of them to bring it up. It was Ginny who finally broke the awkward silence.

"I think maybe we all want to know about the other…ummm…odd behavior," said Ginny.

"What odd behavior?" I asked.

"Dude, you hissed," said Eric.

"Hissed?" I asked.

They all nodded.

"There's more," said Ginny. "You stood over the bodies and flicked your tongue like a snake scenting the air," said Ginny. "It was creepy."

I was stunned. Ginny looked at me like she had just learned some terrible truth about a loved one and didn't know what to make of it.

Eric nodded and asked, "What's gotten into you?"

Marguerite looked thoughtful.

This was all news to me. I didn't remember any of it. I wanted to say something to reassure them. Instead, I stood there staring at them, feeling cold and empty.

"Afterwards, you crumbled to the ground and began shaking," said Pony Tail. "Do you have a history of seizures?"

I shook my head.

"What happened when you killed the Anaconda?" asked Marguerite.

"Not much really," I answered. "I was losing the fight. The damn thing was squeezing the life out of me and I couldn't breathe. In desperation I stabbed a finger as far as I could into the serpent's eye socket and then passed out."

"Grant, this is important," said Marguerite. "Did anything else happen before you passed out?"

"Yeah, I was consumed by white light, followed by darkness," I answered. "I think I died. At least I thought I was dead. I kept looking for Dad. I wanted him to guide me to the other side, but he never showed up. I was alone."

In barely a whisper Ginny said, "You're not alone."

Eric put his arm around me and rumpled my hair.

"Did anything happen before you saw the white light?" asked Marguerite.

At first I couldn't think of anything so I returned to the experience and played it slowly out in my mind. Then I remembered.

"There was a shock," I said. "It felt like I touched an exposed wire with my finger, but it was cold, intensely cold. The cold ran down my arm to the base of my spine. There it gathered in a pool. Something heated it, until it churned like molten lava. Then it shot up my spine. When it reached my crown it exploded into white light. I don't remember anything after that except darkness. All of this happened in the blink of an eye."

"Hurry everyone," said Marguerite. "Time is of the essence. We must see the Council immediately."

"What Council?" I asked.

She didn't answer. Motioning for us to follow, she headed deeper into the rainforest. Hoping for an answer, I cut my eyes to Ginny, but all I got from her was a shrug. There was nothing to do but follow Marguerite deeper into the rainforest.

The sounds of battle could be heard all around us. Since Marguerite was in a hurry, I figured we would move quickly through the jungle, but in stealth mode. Instead, Marguerite acted like she was on a Sunday stroll in the park and didn't have a care in the world.

Every time the gunfire drew near, I expected

us to drop to the ground and survey our position, but instead we marched steadily on without changing course. Eventually the gunfire stopped and all we could hear were the voices of rainforest creatures. I liked it much better than the violence we left behind.

The rainforest is a living thing. Scientists believe they can understand it by cataloging the diverse plants and animals who call it home. That doesn't really work. The only way to understand the rainforest is to embrace the whole thing. It cannot be dissected.

Not that we could see much of it in the dark thanks to a thick canopy that blocked most of the night sky. Still, our eyes somehow adjusted to the limited light, revealing just enough of the shadowy forest that we somehow maneuvered our way through it without incident.

We hiked all night. Even though the forest floor was soft with damp leaves, it was not an easy hike in bare feet. I was grateful when we took a break just as the morning sun peeked through a gap in the leaves.

Marguerite stopped. She took a long slow deep breath and told us we were almost there.

I couldn't see it, but I heard running water. Marguerite led us to a bubbling stream where we took refreshment and renewed ourselves. After taking a long drink of water, Pony Tail fell fast asleep. Eric sat with his back to a tree and watched the sun rise through a break in the foliage. Ginny rested on a flat rock and dipped her feet in the water.

I took a few minutes to marvel at the flowers. The way they grow both on the ground and in the trees gave this place a fairy tale atmosphere that Ginny seemed to fit into perfectly. I was thinking how perfectly she fit into my life as well when I sat down next to her on the rock, but she stiffened and leaned away from me.

Not a good sign, I thought. She hadn't been the same since my killing spree. I wanted to say something that would make it all better, but nothing came to mind.

She felt so distant and I didn't know how to bridge the gap between us. To make matters worse, I was divided against myself. I knew if I didn't fix it, I was lost. I remember Ch'ing telling me that when things aren't going right all you have to do is return to your ground. I didn't know what the hell that meant, but I did feel the urge to do Tai Chi.

I stood up and stepped into the water. Facing upstream, I could see a mountain in the distance. For some reason it soothed me. Taking a deep breath, I imagined I was drawing the mountain into me. It felt good, so I did it again and again, until every cell of my body was filled with vital energy.

One morning I found Ch'ing doing the opening movement of Tai Chi, over and over again. It is a very simple posture called, "Spreading a Silk Sheet." I was about to ask why he didn't continue with the full set but he spoke first.

"If I can only get this right, then I will return to a state of balance," said Ch'ing.

I thought he was joking. Ch'ing is a Master. It's the simplest movement to learn in Tai Chi. How could such a simple repetitive exercise restore his balance? Anyway, he seemed pretty balanced to me.

On the other hand, my life was way out of balance. I wondered if Ch'ing's exercise would work for me and decided to give it a try.

I began by slowly drawing my hands up and catching the air under an imaginary silk sheet. In coordination with my rising hands, I drew air into my lungs and then used it to fill the space under the billowing sheet.

When it reached its apex, the floating sheet was spread wide above the king sized bed and my lungs were expanded to the max with oxygen rich air. Then and only then, did I slowly begin to exhale. Without air to support it, the sheet floated gently to the surface of the bed.

Not satisfied with the way it spread, I repeated the exercise over and over again. With each repetition, I softened and rounded the movement and worked to make my breath as smooth as a silkworm pulling its fragile thread.

Something strange began to happen. At times I was the sheet. At other times, I was the bed. It wasn't until I knew that the sheet, the bed, and I were the same, did I finally get it right. I felt an incredible peace spread through me.

I don't know how long I rested in this peaceful state, but the serenity was interrupted by a chill. It began in my feet and slowly crept up my legs. Hungering for the warm fuzzy feeling I just enjoyed during meditation, I ignored it, but the cold wouldn't go away. It continued its relentless march up my back. I was exposed and wished there was something to cover my nakedness.

I hate being cold. Ch'ing knew this about me, so he would teach us outdoors in the dead of winter. The first time it happened, Eric and I awoke to a heavy snow storm one morning and planned to do some sledding on Hippie Hill. We covered ourselves from head to toe in layers of warm clothing and headed out.

Ch'ing caught us on the way out the door.

Seeing our heavy clothing, he sadly shook his head and announced it was time for a lesson. He sent us back into the house with instructions to remove all of our useless winter clothing.

Eric looked at me and groaned.

I whispered, "This can't be good."

We reluctantly removed our winter coats, gloves and hats, but kept our sweaters and jeans. Much to our dismay, Ch'ing insisted we remove those as well.

I did not want to take my clothes off. My mind raced as I formulated a list of excuses to avoid following Ch'ing's instructions. It wasn't so much the cold that concerned me, although that was certainly a problem. Nudity just wasn't something I did in public.

Ch'ing had been like a father to me. I loved and trusted him. The thought of disappointing him was unbearable. Still, it wasn't until I realized that I was about to disappoint myself, that I found the courage to remove my clothes and step outside. It was the hardest thing I had ever done.

Shifu found the deepest snow bank to begin class. Standing naked in the snow, it didn't take long before our teeth were chattering.

With a grin Ch'ing said, "So you boys think you're cold."

I was cold and my chattering teeth proved it.

"I bet you wish you had all those clothes right now to keep you warm," said Ch'ing.

Our heads bobbed up and down in agreement.

"There is an endless supply of heat inside of you," said Ch'ing. "I'm going to show you how to connect with it. So listen up."

Ch'ing paused for dramatic effect. When he was satisfied we were listening, he continued.

"Close your eyes," said Ch'ing. "Take a long deep breath. Then another one and another one until you begin to feel the fire in your belly."

It didn't take long before I began to feel the fire in my belly. Grasping at the warmth it provided, I let it spread throughout my body. I clung to it until I felt the first beads of sweat dripping from my forehead. It was then that Ch'ing told us to open our eyes.

Ch'ing's eyes twinkle when he's about to teach us a hard life lesson.

"You boys need to learn how to look at your naked selves," he said.

Eric looked at me and snickered. I wasn't quite so amused. Looking at naked girls is pretty much all two teenage boys ever think about, but there was nothing exciting about standing outside in the cold snow in nothing but our birthday suits.

Ch'ing rolled his eyes and said, "If you two perverts can manage to control your hormones, I will continue your lesson."

When we finally stopped giggling, Ch'ing continued.

"Right now, I bet you think I'm talking about your physical bodies," he said.

Of course that's what we thought he meant by naked selves and nodded in unison.

"Noooo, not at all," said Ch'ing. "So, if it's not the obvious, then what do you think I might be talking about?"

When we didn't answer, Ch'ing pointed to Eric and asked, "Eric, what's left when you eliminate the obvious?"

Eric hated answering questions in class and usually responded with a wise crack. This was no different.

"Umm, are you talking about my stash of girlie magazines?" asked Eric.

"Always the irreverent one, aren't you, Eric?" said Ch'ing. "I'm talking about your authentic selves."

He paused and studied us closely before continuing.

"There I go again using big words with lots of syllables," said Ch'ing. "If you pay attention, you boys might learn something yet. I'm not talking about your skin. What is real about each of you is beneath your skin."

Once again he waited and watched.

"The only way to see your naked body is to strip away all the layers of clothing," said Ch'ing. "Well guess what? Your real selves are covered with layers of bullshit and lies. The only way to see it is to strip away the layers of self-deception. Let me warn you boys. It takes tremendous courage."

"The shivering you were doing earlier didn't have anything to do with today's temperature," said Ch'ing. "You were shivering because you're just scared little boys right now. If you want to grow into the men I know you can become, then you must have the guts to be honest with yourselves and strip away the stories you tell yourselves about yourselves. Do you understand?"

I figured I was pretty honest. About the only thing I lied about was what I was really doing for all that time in the bathroom. Touching myself several times a day wasn't something I could easily talk about. Especially since it was plain ole' Ginny I thought about when I was doing it.

Ch'ing continued his lesson, "Today, I'm going to give you the tools you need. It will be up to you to know when to use them."

Ch'ing gave us a conspiratorial look and lowered his voice, "I bet you didn't know there are a bunch of crazy monks in the Himalayas who sit naked in the snow during meditation. The mountain wind can be brutal up there. They have nothing but their inner fire to warm themselves. As if being naked isn't enough, they spread wet cloth across their backs to dry. They measure their skill by the number of towels they can dry and the size of the puddle created from the snow they melt."

Eric and I looked at each other. Now this was some cool shit. He had our undivided attention and we were hanging on every word.

With his typical dramatic flair, Ch'ing waited patiently until we asked, "How do they do that?"

He grinned. "Well I'm glad you asked. I'm going to teach you how to do it. One day you will come face to face with your naked self. When you do, you will feel cold even though it's warm out. Don't be fooled. Your shivers are fear, nothing more. The truth can be scary as hell."

As I stood there shivering in the middle of the stream, I knew what I needed to do. It was time to be honest with myself. For some reason, I was afraid to open my eyes. Thinking of the monks sitting in the snow, I began the mediation

Ch'ing taught us so long ago.

The warmth was comforting. When I was ready, I opened my eyes. I was staring into a pool of water. The reflection was unfocused at first. When it cleared, I nearly fell backwards. It wasn't me I saw reflected in the water. It was the Anaconda and its mouth was wide open to attack.

I couldn't move. It was as if my legs were buried beneath me. There was nothing I could do but continue the meditation. I stoked the inner fire to a blaze. The Anaconda wasn't daunted, but it didn't attack either. It waited. Then I knew what I had to do. I wrapped my arms around it and hugged.

Now I understood. Something happened when I jabbed my finger into its brain. I felt a jolt of electricity. Something passed from the great reptile to me. It awoke something inside of me. It drove me to satisfy my base needs, first and foremost. Kill or be killed. Eat or starve. Fuck or forever die. The cold blooded reptile was inside of me and I accepted it.

My peace returned. I was drifting in a void where I felt nothing, heard nothing, saw nothing and thought nothing. I don't know how long I was there, but it was interrupted by a beautiful sound…it was laughter. It was a good sound. I was drawn to it. I followed it to the source. It was the sound of joy. It was my joy. The laughter came from a deep place inside of me.

When I thought I was all but laughed out, I opened my eyes. Something had shifted. I was the mountain, the stream, and the rainforest. A hand touched my arm. Without looking, I knew it was Ginny. Nothing was said. Nothing needed to be said. What needed to be said was communicated by the touch. All was well between us.

It was then I heard the distinctive sound of a gun bolt loading a fresh round into the chamber. We had been discovered.

CHAPTER 16

It wasn't just one soldier, it was a whole squad, and that was a lot of damn guns in our faces. The Stone Age battle axe I carried all night was now propped against a tree three paces away. Not that it would have made much difference anyway. Its range is a bit shorter than the squad's M4A1 automatic weapons.

I didn't like the way they were looking at Ginny and had a sinking feeling this wasn't going to end well. These men looked like they had been in the bush too long and they were accustomed to taking what they wanted, especially when it came to women. This naturism thing has a few drawbacks.

The only hope I had was the possibility the rest of our group hadn't been discovered and they would somehow slip in behind the soldiers. If that happened, then we might have a slim chance of surviving the impending battle. Whether we got help or not, I planned to fight to the death before I let them harm Ginny.

They were dressed in camouflage pattern

pants, shirts and vests loaded with pockets. Their heads were covered with matching patrol caps, but their combat boots were tan. None of the uniforms had any identifying patches that I could see.

I guess the money they saved on patches went into their guns. The rifles were the latest military issue automatic weapons loaded with a variety of special operations modifications. Things like aiming lasers, illuminators, and grenade launchers. These guys were serious about their guns.

I was about to ask them what they wanted, when Ginny spoke.

"What are you doing?" she demanded.

No one answered, so Ginny tried again.

"You men work for me," she said.

There was no response.

"Philippe, lower that weapon and explain yourself," ordered Ginny.

He must have been the short guy on the right flank because his eyes showed the first signs of doubt as he looked to see what the rest of the squad was going to do.

Ginny took advantage of this weakness and said, "Raul, tell Philippe to lower his weapon."

Raul must have been the guy standing next to Philippe, because he opened his mouth to comply with Ginny's order, but was interrupted by the sound of an approaching helicopter and then snapped it shut again. His face was conflicted, but the last thing I saw flash cross it just before it went stone blank again was sheer terror.

The progress Ginny made softening them was wiped away in an instant. Each soldier, without exception, went hard and cold. They feared whoever was in the whirly bird more than her.

There was nothing to do but wait, but the wait didn't last long. The Apache attack helicopter is fast and it was on the ground within minutes. I didn't think the soldiers faces could get any more grim, but when the helicopter engine shut down, they proved me wrong.

I wasn't sure what to expect, but when the door opened I sure wasn't expecting to see a flamboyant pipsqueak hit the ground with a bounce. He couldn't have been more than 5'2" and 110 pounds soaking wet.

He was dressed like a flamer, with lime green yoga pants and an orange blouse, opened wide to the navel. Hanging between his pierced nipples was a black onyx necklace. There was a touch of black mascara on his lips and at the corners of his eyes.

Ch'ing taught me to never underestimate

people, but this guy did not fit my idea of what a villain should look like. I have to confess, I felt cheated. Still, he made a grand entrance and I couldn't help but wonder who the hell he was.

The fop strutted over to us like a little banty rooster with his chest all puffed out. He thought he was something special, but I wasn't seeing it. He stopped a couple of paces in front of us and looked me up and down. Actually, it was more down than up and it made me uncomfortable that he stared so openly at my junk.

"Victor, what the hell are you doing?" demanded Ginny.

Victor reluctantly turned his attention to Ginny and said with a sigh, "Why isn't it obvious, I'm staging a coup?"

"A coup...I don't understand," said Ginny.

"Don't be a bore," said Victor. "You're smarter than that."

I wasn't about to let him insult Ginny and asked, "Do I know you?"

"My name is Victor Branco," he answered.

Victor Branco was Ginny's head of security and I had a few questions I wanted to ask him.

"Why did you hire me to guard, Padma?" I asked.

"Oh, is that the best you've got?" he asked with an exaggerated yawn. "I'm disappointed in you, my yummy hunk. I was expecting something more probing from you than that. If you must know, I was following orders."

"On whose orders?" I asked.

"Oh…well…now that's the question, isn't it?" he replied.

"You're not going to tell me, are you?" I asked.

Victor shook his head and added, "Nope."

"I'm the one who signs your pay check, Victor," said Ginny. "It wasn't my orders."

"You again," said Victor with a sigh. "I love being the one to tell you this, but you're such a small player on this game board, my bitch of an ex-boss."

Ginny's eyes blazed and her face flushed red, but her voice was cold, very cold, as she said, "Ex is right you little prick."

Victor smirked, "Oh dear…little prick she says. You know so little about me, you arrogant bitch. I may be short of stature, but I'm hung like a donkey. Would you care to see it?"

It was me he was looking at when he asked the question, but I sure as hell wasn't taking that bait.

"I'll pass," I said. "I have one of my own, but I would like to know how you found us in the middle of this vast jungle?"

Victor looked genuinely disappointed. I

thought maybe he might press the point, but instead he let out a little bark. At least it sounded like a bark, but you know how it is when something happens that is too incongruent to believe. First we do a double take and then reinvent what happened. I decided it was a snort laugh and not a bark at all.

"Oh, that was easy," said Victor. "I'm her chief of security and one of her most trusted employees. I have complete access to her. I just replaced her belly button rings with tracking devices."

"Tracking devices," I said.

"Yes…yes…I've been following her movements for years," he said

"Why would you follow me?" asked Ginny.

"I've been waiting for you to lead us to your father," he said.

"What do you want with my father?" asked Ginny.

"It's not what I want," answered Victor. "It's what my employer wants."

"And, you're not going to tell us who that is," I said.

He shook his head.

"It doesn't matter," I said. "I know who you work for."

"Nice try, but you don't know shit," said

Victor.

"Wilbur Goth, Pathogen's psycho CEO, thinks Bill Bardough can lead him to a special healing plant," I said. "The real question is why you betrayed Ginny for that piece of shit."

Victor rubbed the back of his neck with his left hand and let out a long hissing breath. He looked at me and then at Ginny. He shook his head and then turned to the helicopter pilot and waived him toward us.

The pilot hustled over and Victor whispered something to him. The pilot sprinted back to the helicopter, rummaged around inside for something and then returned with a satellite phone that he handed to Victor.

Victor punched in a number and said, "I have them, but there's something you should know. They know more than we realized."

He paused and listened before saying, "They know who you are and what you want."

He listened for a bit and then hung up.

"Kill 'em," he said.

Philippe turned to Victor, "Sir…"

Ginny stretched a desperate hand toward the soldiers, "Don't do this. I beg you."

Everyone froze.

Victor exploded, "That was an ORDER!"

The soldiers refocused with grim

determination. Whatever hold Victor had over them was bigger than anything Ginny could surmount. These men were going to kill us.

That's pretty much when all hell broke loose. Of all the people to save us, I never expected it to be the slavers. A band of men with the telltale tattoo around their biceps sprang from the bushes and attacked the soldiers with machetes.

We used the diversion to sprint for cover. While we escaped Victor and the squad, we stumbled onto a second group of soldiers holding Eric and the others hostage. Fortunately, we had flanked them and as they tried to turn toward us, Eric sprang into action with Marguerite and Pony Tail right behind him.

This time I felt the serpent inside of me and we fought as one to destroy our enemies. Only one of the soldiers managed to slip away. Once we finished with his mates, we fled back into the rainforest.

CHAPTER 17

Marguerite led us upstream toward the mountain. When we came to white water cascading around huge boulders covered in lime green moss, we left the stream to make our way through the thick undergrowth. It was a trail I would not have attempted to blaze on my own, but thanks to Marguerite's leadership we wove our way through it with effortless grace.

When we finally broke through the brush, the character of the forest changed. The trees got bigger, way bigger in fact. I didn't recognize the variety, but they were comparable to the California sequoia in size.

At first I thought the bark on these massive trees had brown and black stripes, but when I got a closer look I saw that it was actually corrugated. The ruts were deep and wide, maybe the length of my forearm. Their branches drooped like a weeping willow as if these trees wanted to claim all of the light their space offered.

They also housed a particularly ugly variety of vultures. The sight of these bottom feeders didn't portend well. I figured, all we needed were skull and crossbones to complete the message we weren't welcome here.

Marguerite ignored the vultures and led us through a natural arch surrounded by a misty haze. I had seen many such arches in the Daniel Boone National Forest, but this one was much taller and more narrow than those in the mountains of Eastern Kentucky.

Beyond the arch, we rapidly gained elevation. As we climbed the mist thickened into a heavy fog making visibility on the narrow mountain trail difficult and treacherous.

One misstep could mean a fall of several hundred feet. While I do not generally fear heights, the risk of a deadly fall was enough to make me hyper vigilant about where I stepped. Unfortunately, the pursuit pressured us to push forward as quickly as possible.

Gunfire popped behind us. Our pursuers had not give up and it sounded like they were gaining ground. Despite our cautiousness, Ginny seemed to have the most trouble. When we heard voices behind us she slipped on loose rock. I caught her in the nick of time or she would have fallen to her death.

Despite the fog we managed to make our way without getting killed. Bullets kicked up dust at our feet making trail visibility even more challenging. When we were nearly to the top, the trail ended at a rock outcropping. To make matters worse, Marguerite circled to the right of it and disappeared into the face of the mountain. In unison, we all turned to Pony Tail in hopes of an explanation.

He shrugged.

"I've never been here before," said Pony Tail.

Ginny's curiosity got the best of her. She cautiously approached the spot where Marguerite disappeared. Just in case, I followed close behind to make sure she stayed safe. There was a shallow crevice too small to fit into. Ginny began to feel around with her hands. Her arm disappeared into the shadows. She turned around and grinned at us.

"It's an illusion," she said. "The shadows hide a cave entrance."

To see better, I moved a little closer. Sure enough, I saw an arched opening that was clearly man made. There were markings on the stone. At first, it appeared to be ornate decoration. I studied it more closely and saw it was a single word, "Unity." Actually, it wasn't written in English at all and I'm not exactly certain how I knew what it said, I just did.

"We better hurry," said Pony Tail. "The

pursuit is closing fast."

We slipped inside and found Marguerite waiting for us. I expected a dark cavern, but instead the arched doorway opened into a well-lit passageway. As far as I could tell, there was no visible source of light. The floor and the walls were lined with polished stone.

Ginny voiced my thoughts.

"This isn't a cave," she said. "What is this place?"

Pony Tail's voice was filled with awe as he replied, "The Temple of the Gods."

"We're inside an ancient pyramid," said Marguerite.

"Is it Mayan?" I asked.

"No, it's much older," answered Marguerite. "Come, follow me."

She led us down a corridor that opened into a large area the size of a city block. At the center of the room was a huge hole in the floor. You could have dropped an office building into it. Marguerite walked in the direction of the hole and then fell.

"Marguerite!" shouted Ginny.

I was stunned and should have paid closer attention to Ginny. She dashed after Marguerite and disappeared into the cavernous pit. A high-pitched scream echoed throughout the cavern.

My stomach flipped and bile burned its way to the back of my throat. There was no time for despair. I couldn't lose her now and rushed toward the spot where she disappeared.

There I found Marguerite and Ginny waiting for us on the steps of a spiraling staircase. Up close, the hole looked like a giant well. It was perfectly symmetrical. Like the passageway, the walls were polished smooth. I didn't see any sign of the bottom. The damn thing seemed to go on forever.

Eric threw his arm over my shoulder.

"Dude, you screamed like a little girl," said Eric.

I didn't realize I was the source of the scream, but it didn't surprise me. I thought I'd lost Ginny. I took her hands and squeezed gently.

"I'm sorry I scared you," she said.

If my hands had been free I would have used them to wipe the tears from my eyes. Instead, I let them run their course unimpeded and contented myself with the knowledge that Ginny was unharmed.

It was Marguerite who broke the spell.

"Hurry," she said.

Marguerite led us in a counter clockwise descent into the bottomless pit. Deeper and deeper we went into the belly of the Earth. I kept thinking it would end soon, but she marched on. The descent was so long, I began to imagine we were headed straight to hell and expected the temperature to rise as we approached the Earth's core, but it remained constant.

I was looking into the pit for signs of fire and brimstone when Marguerite made a sharp turn to the right. It was another passageway. Before I stepped into it, I took one last look at the hole. There was no sign of the bottom. I couldn't help but wonder where the hell it went.

At the end of the long passageway was an arched doorway leading into an eight sided chamber. At its center was a pool of water. On each face of the octagon sat an empty throne marked with a trigram of the I Ching.

The I Ching is an ancient Chinese text that is usually translated as the Book of Changes. It is typically thought of as a book of divinity or fortune telling. Ch'ing once told me that trying to use it to predict the future misses the mark. He said it is a blueprint of life and nothing more. Geez, as if understanding life is nothing. Ch'ing is such a master of understatement.

My eyes were drawn to the pool of water. There was the outline of a symbol the Taoist call The Grand Terminus. Most westerners call it the yin-yang symbol. It is a reminder that opposites must exist in a balanced state. When you deny one or the other, then nature will work to restore balance.

We are not what other people want us to be. When we accept ourselves as we are, then we can move through life's changes until balance is restored. Then and only then can we live an authentic life. Living life on our own terms is the great end.

My thoughts were interrupted by footsteps coming from the hallway we had just exited. Pony Tail spun around and dropped to a crouch. Eric slipped over and took a position on the opposite side of the archway.

Pony Tail growled in a low voice, "Our enemies have followed us into this sacred place."

Ginny dug her nails into my upper arm. I can't be certain, but I think she drew blood. She leaned toward me and whispered.

"What do we do now, Grant?"

"We fight," I answered.

"Let 'em come," snarled Eric.

All eyes were fixed on the archway. The footsteps suddenly stopped and the passage beyond the archway grew silent. There was nothing to do, but wait and breathe. I took a long slow breath and waited with Ginny at my side.

None of us had weapons. They had been taken by Victor's men. We had no choice but to face the enemy with bare hands, strong hearts, and our wits.

It wasn't as bad as it seemed. Guns gain you an advantage when there is distance between you and your enemy. In close quarters, the advantage is lost. Besides, the ultimate weapon in any fight is the mind. The man with the greater will to survive usually does.

It came at us fast and high. I couldn't quite make it out, but was thinking it looked vaguely familiar when I heard a squawk.

"Aaawk," squawked Bird. "Do not fear! It is I, Ponce de Leon."

Bird landed softly on my shoulder and rubbed the back of his head on my cheek. I was lost for words. Bird never shows me affection.

"It's you, Bird," I mumbled.

"Aaawk, damn right baby," said Bird. "It doesn't get any better than this."

Bird turned his attention to Ginny.

"Aaawk, hey there sexy girl," he said.

Ginny purred, "Oh Bird."

Bird moved to Ginny's shoulder and gave her a rub on the cheek.

With a lecherous bird beak grin he squawked, "Aaawk, naked gooood and you wear it so well."

Ginny looked startled and took a quick look down at herself. Before she could respond Bird hopped to Marguerite's shoulder. She reached up and stroked his feathers. It was Bird's turn to purr.

"It's been too long Ponce," said Marguerite. "I've missed you."

Bird was uncharacteristically quiet.

"Can't that old fool keep up with you?" asked Marguerite.

Bird's dramatic entrance had completely distracted us from the footsteps. When we returned our attention to the archway, we found Padma standing there looking the part of a Christmas elf in his red robe and green cowboy boots.

Padma's smile was sweet and his eyes twinkled. For just an instant, I thought he might actually be Santa.

"Old fool!" said Padma. "Is that any way to speak to someone of my stature?"

Marguerite laughed as she pointed at his round belly.

"Your stature has grown substantially since we last saw each other," said Marguerite. "You've added another half a Padma to your already prominent self."

Padma giggled like a school girl.

"There just isn't enough of me to go around," said Padma.

Marguerite spread her arms wide.

"Come give me a proper greeting, dearest," said Marguerite.

Padma strolled over and wrapped her up in a big ole bear hug. When they finished, he did the same with the rest of us. I wanted to ask him about his disappearance, but he spoke first.

"There will be time for questions later," said Padma. "I must make a few preparations before Council begins. Please make yourselves comfortable."

After Padma left, Marguerite took a seat on one of the thrones. I glanced at the markings at her feet and saw it was the symbol for Earth. Bird flew over and perched on one of the thrones. It was marked Wind.

Curious about the yin-yang symbol in the pool, I walked over to get a closer look. Ginny followed me. Pony Tail and Eric remained posted at the doorway like a couple of palace guards.

The water was crystal clear. There was no bottom in sight. The symbol seemed to float on the surface. It was also slowly rotating counter clockwise. There was writing engraved around the edge of the pool. I followed the lettering and read, "From This Pool Springs Eternal Life."

I was about to share it with Ginny when she stepped into the water. What the hell! My stomach flipped and I lunged for her but it was too late. Instead of sinking, she walked across the water and came to a rest at the center.

Standing on the yin-yang symbol, she beckoned me to come to her. There must be stepping stones. I looked at the path she took and saw no sign of them. I wanted to join her, but I didn't know how the hell she did it.

A thought popped into my head, "Suspend reason. Trust her."

I took a deep breath and gazed into Ginny's eyes. What I saw was unconditional love. I allowed it to push the doubt aside. Choosing trust, I stepped into the water.

Never once taking my eyes off of her, I walked across the surface of the pool and joined Ginny at the center. Standing face to face, she took both of my hands into her own. All awareness of our surroundings disappeared. We stood silent and never once wavered.

I have no idea how long we stood there wrapped in love. Gradually, the chamber reappeared. I was surprised to see all eight of the thrones filled and damned if Padma didn't rest comfortably in one of the seats. I was even more surprised to see Marguerite and Bird still seated. However, nothing matched the shock of seeing Ch'ing.

"Ch'ing", I whispered.

Shifu had disappeared without a trace from his home. The house had been ransacked. Eric and I didn't have a clue what happened to him and feared the worst. I thought we had lost him. Of all the places for Ch'ing to turn up, I never expected it to be deep in the belly of the Earth.

I caught Eric's eye and we nodded to each other. A wave of gratitude spread through me.

A round black woman with a kind face began the discussion.

"It is time," she said. "Long ago there was a break in the circle. A prophesy followed. An era of suffering will spread across the Earth like a pestilence. People will lose themselves. They will know only fear and violence. Many lies will be told to them to mask their illness. When all hope is lost, two acting as one will rise to the top and heal them."

A giant of a man pointed toward us and said in a deep baritone voice, "Eve are you satisfied they are the ones?"

All eyes turned to us. I wanted to ask Ch'ing what the hell was going on, but something in his expression stopped me. There was nothing to do but wait.

A beautiful young woman with waves of golden hair responded in an angelic voice, "I am not convinced."

To my surprise Eve's seat was marked with the trigram representing Heaven. It is the symbol for creativity, but it also represents the risks of being head strong.

"The water accepted them," said Marguerite.

"He stands in the feminine and she stands in the masculine," said Ch'ing.

I glanced down. The light half of the yin-yang symbol represents masculine energy. Ginny was standing within it. The dark half represents the feminine counterpart and there I stood.

Padma added, "More importantly, they stand as one."

Eve wasn't about to concede and said, "There remains one more test."

Ch'ing slumped in his seat. Marguerite stiffened. They looked very concerned. This can't be good. I was surprised to hear Bird speak without his usual squawk.

"Please don't do this Eve," said Bird.

Eve may have been the most petite among them, but at this moment she seemed to tower over the others.

Smelling victory she said, "What's the matter

Ponce? Are you afraid your pets won't survive it?"

What did she mean…survive it? The test must be dangerous. The thought of loosing Ginny was unbearable. I opened my mouth to protest, but was interrupted by a shout from Bird.

"I'm not afraid," said Bird. "It's just…"

He in turn was interrupted by the Giant's booming voice, "Eve, you have gone too far this time."

Eve looked pleased with herself. I doubt she agreed she had gone too far at all.

In a soothing tone Layah said, "Relax everyone. Eve, I see no reason to put them to the test. All we need is someone capable of bringing Great Mother to market."

The Prophesy Lady said, "It will be no easy task to bring this medicine to the world. They will face resistance on many fronts. It will be extremely dangerous. We need to know if they have what it takes to accomplish this task. I agree with Eve. They must face the final test."

Eve moved in for the kill.

"Listen to Delphoria," said Eve. "Billions of dollars are at stake. This medicine will make us all very rich."

Rich…is this all about the money? They have the ability to heal and all they think about is getting rich. Great Mother can end the world's suffering. My God, what we could accomplish if we solved the health care crisis. We could move into a Golden Age. Exploiting the world's suffering is just more of the same. Shame on them.

That's when it occurred to me that if I turned my back on the Council, then I might never be able to give the medicine to my mother. I had a moment of self-doubt. If I did what they wanted, then I could save my mother. I thought about Pathogen's evil plans and it occurred to me that to fight the rich and powerful I needed to be rich and powerful too.

It was tempting, very tempting.

I turned away from the Council and focused all of my attention on Ginny. Her eyes were filled with tears. In those tears I found myself. The course was clear. Together we spoke, two voices as one.

"No," we said. "We will not do this for you. This medicine cannot be sold. We will not profit from the suffering of others. Great Mother must be given freely to everyone."

There was a long stretch of silence. I figured we had failed the test. They would probably throw us out and that would be the end of it.

It was Eve who finally spoke up.

"Congratulations," she said. "You have passed the final test."

"A new era begins," said the Giant.

"It is time for the two of you to spread Great Mother to the four corners of the world," said Ch'ing.

The Council members rose from their thrones and began to dance. It was a dance of joy.

It took a moment, but then I understood. The final test was the lure of unimaginable wealth. At the edge of the pool was a small plant in a simple earthen pot. They had given us Great Mother.

The plant drew us across the surface of the water, and we were almost to it, when gun fire exploded in the chamber. I forgot Great Mother and pulled Ginny to safety. Once we were both flat on the ground, I surveyed the room. Eric and Pony Tail stood with their arms in the air. Behind each of them stood a soldier with a weapon jammed into the center of their backs.

Victor pointed a gun toward the plant and said, "I'll take that."

The weird thing was the Council members were still dancing around their thrones. It was as if they hadn't heard the gun fire. Victor was stammering and sputtering indignantly at their odd behavior. When his patience finally ran out, he turned the gun on them.

"You freaks need to stop that weird shit and die with some damn dignity," screamed Victor.

At that very instant, the light went out and the chamber became pitch black. I heard Ch'ing's voice close to my ear.

"It is time to leave," said Ch'ing. "Take my hand."

# # #

Thank you for reading my book. Won't you please take a moment to leave a book review at your favorite retailer?

Peace out,
Robert

CONTINUE THE ADVENTURE

We hope you enjoyed reading *Nostrum Conspiracy*. Continue the adventure with Robert's third book, *UnderBelly*.

You will also love Robert's first book, *Naked Tao*.

What Others are Saying About *Naked Tao*:

"A very enjoyable read. Really looking forward to the sequel." A. Engle

"I witnessed the cosmic dance and laughed out loud! A provocative and assumption shattering piece of work." Christopher Gray

"A fast paced, quick, entertaining read, that is balanced with story line twists and emotional struggle." Jeremy Nicheols.

UNDERBELLY

SAMPLE CHAPTER

CHAPTER 1

They say your senses heighten when one is lost. It went pitch black right after Victor threatened to shoot everybody, so maybe fear had something to do with it as well. Whatever the explanation might be, I heard a symphony of heartbeat and breathe, accompanied by the tap and shuffle of dancing feet playing in the darkness.

"Turn on the damn lights," shouted Victor.

"It is time to leave," whispered Ch'ing.

Victor blocked the only entrance to the chamber. Since he was armed with an automatic weapon, it didn't seem possible we could get past him. Sifu is like a father to me and I trust him with my life. If he says it's time to leave, then he has a way out. I was ready, but wasn't going anywhere without Ginny.

Victor was once Ginny's most trusted employee. The traitor now works for the pharmaceutical giant, Pathogen. He tracked us across continents and into the belly of the Earth. Thanks to the miracles of modern technology, not even a secret chamber hidden far below a lost pyramid is enough to keep him at bay.

He plans to kill us and I'm not sure why he didn't do it when he had the chance. Instead, he opted to profane this sacred place with gunfire. He's a jerk all right, but Victor's need for a dramatic entrance has cost him the kill…so far.

We dove for cover when he blasted off a round, but other than the cover of darkness, there isn't much to hide behind. Council chambers is an eight sided room carved out of stone. On each face sits a marble throne. In the center is a pool of clear water that has no bottom the eye can see.

The dancing feet belong to an ancient council. They are a hodgepodge of the strangest characters you have ever laid eyes upon and they have an even stranger agenda. Just before Victor made his dramatic appearance, they delivered a powerful new medicine to Ginny and me on the condition we freely spread it across the world.

There's just one problem. Victor's new boss, Wilbur Goth, C.E.O. of Pathogen, wants the medicine for himself and he will do anything to stop us. It was Goth who ordered Victor to kill us.

My name is Grant Li. Up until a few days ago I had a promising legal career ahead of me, but now I'm an unemployed attorney. In my first big case, I defended Goth against charges that he intentionally deceived the public about the risks of Gutchriem, an acid-reflux medicine that is believed to be killing people. I won the case, but now there is new evidence that Gutchriem is laced with a deadly virus.

Ginny Bardough is a childhood friend and my one true love. Up until a few days ago, it had been years since we had last seen each. Our reunion has not been easy. So far, we've had to overcome huge obstacles, including our present situation with Victor. If we get out of this alive, I plan to marry her as soon as my divorce is final.

She was lying next to me at the edge of the pool. Not exactly touching, but close enough I could feel strands of her raven hair tickling my shoulder. The polished stone floor was just shy of slippery and surprisingly warm. The scent of gunpowder quickly gave way to a stream of air that smelled as fresh as the blue sky after a summer squall.

Ch'ing is usually relaxed, but I sensed urgency in his whisper, "Take my hand."

"I have enough lead to cover every square inch of this God forsaken hole in the Earth," shouted Victor. "If you don't turn the lights back on like I said, then I'm going to start shooting and I won't stop until every last living thing in here is dead."

I led a lunatic into this sacred place and I knew I should do something about the danger I put everyone in, but Sifu is right. It's time to flee. We need to get home with the medicine. Mom is trapped inside a coma and the nursing home is about to evict her. We also need to stop Pathogen from using a dangerous virus against innocent people.

"Aaawk, bring the babe with you," squawked Bird in a voice loud enough to wake the dead.

Bird is a Macaw I inherited from Dad. It turns out he is more than he seems. He claims his real name is Juan Ponce de León, and I'm starting to believe him, since he is one of the mucky-mucks on the council of elders.

Ginny inched a little closer.

"Give me your hand," I whispered.

She didn't hesitate. Once her hand was firmly in mine, we rose together as quietly as we could. Despite our best efforts, we made enough noise that a stealthy escape was out of the question.

I turned to Ch'ing and whispered, "We're ready. Let's go."

Whether he heard me is hard to say since the room erupted into a second round of gunfire that sent us back peddling. When my heel caught on something hard, I instinctively looked down to see what it could be and caught a glimpse of

Ginny's face in the gun flash.

I thought the shadows were playing tricks on me until I smelled blood mixed with the gun smoke. I'm not sure if the searing pain I felt was from a bullet or the heartache of seeing blood splattered across Ginny's face. Either way, it hurt like hell.

As I fell backwards I could not help but wonder what might have been had I not spent a lifetime avoiding Ginny. I tried to let her go, but she had me in a death grip and pulled with all her might.

Her effort was heroic, but it was not enough. The momentum from the fall, coupled with the dead weight of my body carried us both into the water. I fought it at first. I fought like the dickens for the life we could have together, but the powerful current sucked us down into a spiraling whirlpool of liquid death.

When I had nothing left and the fight was lost, fear began to creep into the corners of my mind. I didn't like it one bit. I might not win the fight against the current, but fear is a product of my mind and therefore, it is something I can control. Instead of fear, I chose to fill my mind with peace.

Once I stopped fighting the whirlpool, I began to notice how it good it felt…like I was wrapped in a liquid cocoon. It was not warm, nor was it cold. It was the perfect temperature, like the womb. It was weird time to think of the womb. At first, I thought it was the beginning of a life review, or could just as easily have been my imagination, but somehow I am certain I could remember the time in my mother's womb.

Every cell felt new and fresh as all that I am began to fall into its proper place. It was pure bliss until I saw Ginny's desperate face close to mine.

I reached for her just as everything began to fade out. The last thing I remember was her lips mashing mine while her tongue forced my mouth open. It was if she was trying to breathe life into me, or then again, maybe it was just a goodbye kiss.

After that, there was nothing until I awoke alone on a tropical beach that sparkled in the sunlight like a field of tiny diamonds. Sand usually makes me feel dirty and has an annoying way of creeping into unwanted places, so when I visit the beach I try to minimize contact with it.

I usually carry a beach chair with me rather than sit on a towel, but for some strange reason I felt an overwhelming urge to roll among these sparkling lights, so that's exactly what I did, rolling haphazardly like a Texas tumbleweed along water's edge.

When I finally rolled to a stop and allowed myself to relax into the sand, it felt like a thousand tiny hands massaged away the old and left me tingling fresh, as if I had just shed an old skin and replaced it with a shiny new me. The diamond beach shredded the false and left a virgin field where a more authentic me could flourish.

There was something special about this place. It was rich and full of infinite possibilities and I was determined to choose among them with the greatest care. Inhaling deeply, I filled my lungs with fresh air and allowed it to nourish the seedlings of change.

It was good to be alive. Allowing the joy to spread into my arms and legs, I stretched them wide and began sweeping sand angels. A nearby sea turtle paused in her nest making, gave me a long frank assessment and then dismissed me as an amateur.

Sea turtles get big, but this girl looked like she had swallowed enough steroids to compete in a bodybuilding contest. She was eighteen feet long and more than twice the size of any sea turtle I had ever seen.

The Ancients revered the tortoise and legend has it that Taoist longevity practices evolved from observations of its slow movements.

Energy cultivation begins with conservation. Chi is not something you should waste. Given everything I had survived lately, I was starting to feel immortal.

I had survived a knife fight with an ex-special forces war hero, got shot in the back, grappled an anaconda with monstrous teeth and went berserker on a machete carrying psycho intent on doing Ginny harm. I don't know how many guns had been pointed in my face before I was flushed down the drain of a lost South American pyramid and landed on this beach.

By all reckoning, I should be dead, and the presence of the sea turtle added to the sense this was part of some personal vision of an afterlife. In the ultimate battle, the tortoise is the Dark Warrior of the North who emerges from the water and escapes the clutches of the Grim Reaper.

Yet, here I was making sand angels next to the mother of all sea turtles. Her presence was no accident. If I had learned nothing else from Ch'ing, the one thing he taught me was to pay attention and never assume events are accidental. The Universe gladly delivers the message we most need to hear. All we have to do is pay attention and the way will become clear.

I took a slow deep breath and focused on a pinpoint of light at the still point of my being. It is from this vantage point that each of us co-creates life with all sentient beings. The stillness expanded until it filled me with emptiness. When I couldn't contain it any longer, peace spilled into the world around me, as it should, since we are all in this together.

When I finally opened my eyes, the sun was overhead and I stared directly into it. For some odd reason, the light didn't hurt my eyes. The teaching that the sun's light will blind us is supported by a lifetime of pain whenever we get too big of a dose. For this reason, I was torn between letting the light in or snapping the lids shut.

This light was softer than usual and it cast a coral tint to the skyline. That would normally mean the day was nearly over, but the sun was straight above so I figured it was high noon.

On the distant horizon, a large bird hitched an updraft to gain elevation. As it spiraled upward, I caught a glimpse of a long tail. Maybe it was a trick of the light, but it was not a bird's tail exactly. Instead, it looked as if belonged to a monkey, but with a fin at the end molded into the shape of a four-faced spearhead.

The bird's cry was haunting, as if the beast was searching for a lost love. Then again, perhaps I was projecting my own feelings onto it. Ginny was still alive. I could feel it and it was time to find her.

ABOUT ROBERT GRANT

Among Robert Grant's many interests are martial arts. He comes from a long line of Taoist, who left their sheltered lives in a mountain monastery to wander a world filled with raw beauty. These wandering monks have a long tradition of telling stories that both entertain and teach. Robert promised his sifu he would keep the tradition of storytelling alive and began developing a story idea that pitted a young lawyer/martial artist against a powerful pharmaceutical company in an epic conflict over a miracle cure. The hero wants to ensure the cure is freely available to everyone, but powerful enemies want to suppress it. It is the story of a young lawyer's call to action in an epic struggle with his former client. He finds love, redemption, and a worthy life purpose. It is an easy fast read with depth and subtle humor. The result is a first-rate thriller with a mystical twist that will have you laughing one minute and crying the next. Come, open a book and let your mind travel to places you never knew existed.

CONNECT WITH ROBERT GRANT

Thank you for reading *Nostrum Conspiracy*. Please tell your friends and family about my work. I am busy writing the next book. If you would like to receive updates on the book launch, book cover contests, and coupons for book pre-orders, then drop me a note at Robert@NTPublishingCompany.com.

Lastly, I want to invite you to come and hang out with me.

Send your mail messages to:
Robert@NTPublishingCompany.com

Follow me on Twitter: https://twitter.com/nakedtao

Like my Facebook page:
http://www.facebook.com/AuthorRobertGrant

Follow me on Google Plus:
https://www.google.com/+RobertGrantNakedTao

Follow my blog at:
http://www.ntpublishingcompany.com

Welcome to our family and please remember to leave a review of *Nostrum Conspiracy*. This book is also available in print at most online retailers.

Peace out,
Robert

ALSO BY ROBERT GRANT

COMING SOON!

GREAT MOTHER

www.ingramcontent.com/pod-product-compliance
Lightning Source LLC
LaVergne TN
LVHW051514070426
835507LV00023B/3110